CW00820808

Holy Attention

Holy Attention

Preaching in Today's Church

Edited by
Frances Ward
and
Richard Sudworth

© The Editors and Contributors 2019

First published in 2019 by the Canterbury Press Norwich
Editorial office
3rd Floor, Invicta House
108–114 Golden Lane
London EC1Y 0TG, UK
www.canterburypress.co.uk

Canterbury Press is an imprint of Hymns Ancient & Modern Ltd
(a registered charity)

Hymns Ancient & Modern® is a registered trademark of Hymns Ancient & Modern Ltd
13A Hellesdon Park Road, Norwich,
Norfolk NR6 5DR, UK

All rights reserved. No part of this publication may be reproduced, stored in a retrieval system, or transmitted, in any form or by any means, electronic, mechanical, photocopying or otherwise, without the prior permission of the publisher, Canterbury Press.

The Authors have asserted their right under the Copyright, Designs and Patents Act 1988 to be identified as the Author of this Work

Where indicated Scripture quotations are from the New Revised Standard Version of the Bible, Anglicized Edition, copyright © 1989, 1995 by the Division of Christian Education of the National Council of the Churches of Christ in the USA. Used by permission. All rights reserved.

Scripture quotations are also from the Revised Standard Version of the Bible, copyright 1946, 1952 and 1971 by the Division of Christian Education of the National Council of the Churches of Christ in the USA. Used by permission. All rights reserved.

British Library Cataloguing in Publication data

A catalogue record for this book is available
from the British Library

978 1 78622 165 0

Printed and bound in Great Britain by CPI Group (UK) Ltd

Contents

Introduction

What grabs and holds the attention today is big business. Cultural commentators and theologians alike describe a world that is information abundant (unlike previous eras) and attention scarce, where our attention is constantly under pressure as a marketable commodity. The attention economy is upon us, where every moment of online activity is subject to clever advertising, designed to make the most of any transaction we make.

That economic pressure is changing what we attend to, and how we attend to it. James Williams was a former Google strategist at the top of his game. He looked around one day and wondered why he and his colleagues – the best brains of his generation – were focused entirely on strategies to develop 'clickbait', sophisticated algorithms designed to persuade – 'hook' – users to come back to a product again and again. There's a four-stage model he and his colleagues used – a trigger, an action, a variable reward, and the user's 'investment' in the product of time or money. The variable reward is the key – it can be a 'surprise', or some other device, designed to create a habit or addiction. Grabbing – and keeping – the attention is what it is all about. And once you're hooked, it's not only your attention that's engaged. Your intention to do, or be, is also compromised. Who hasn't had the experience of playing just one more game, instead of doing the dishes, or getting ready for a meeting, or picking the kids up? Or preparing a sermon?

When it comes to the Web, we think we're spiders, but really we're flies.

Williams gave it all up and went to Oxford to study philosophy and then wrote his 2018 book *Stand Out of Our Light*. There he argues that the next-generation threat to human freedom is the systems of intelligent persuasion that increasingly direct our thoughts and actions. This economy thrives when our attention is distracted, when we are redirected to what we really, really want and forget how to want what we really want to want. When we allow ourselves to be distracted, and stop training ourselves to attend, it can be deeply undermining of the human will, both individually and collectively. Williams writes that we need to reclaim our attention:

> The liberation of the human attention may be the defining moral and political struggle of our time. Its success is prerequisite for the success of virtually all other struggles. We therefore have an obligation to rewire this system of intelligent, adversarial persuasion before it rewires us. Doing so requires hacking together new ways of talking and thinking about the problem, as well as summoning the courage necessary for advancing on it in inconvenient and unpopular ways.[1]

Another social commentator, Matthew Crawford, explores his concern about the amount of attention that's given to the virtual world stimulated in our heads by digital engagement. He speaks of mental lives that are fractured, distracted, rewired by new habits of information grazing and electronic stimulation, to the extent it's hard to give serious, concentrated engagement to anything. We lack 'the sort of guidance that once would have been supplied by tradition, religion, or the kinds of communities that make deep demands on us'.[2]

In *On Consumer Culture*,[3] the priest-theologian Mark Clavier calls the Church to counter the sophisticated rhetoric of the

1 James Williams, *Stand Out of Our Light: Freedom and Resistance in the Attention Economy* (Cambridge: Cambridge University Press, 2018), p. xii.

2 Matthew Crawford, *The World Beyond Your Head: On Becoming an Individual in an Age of Distraction* (New York: Farrar, Straus and Giroux, 2015), pp. 4–5.

3 Mark Clavier, *On Consumer Culture, Identity, The Church and the Rhetorics of Delight* (New York, London: T&T Clark, 2019).

marketplace with a deeper rhetoric that goes to the heart of human desire and delight. Others address the tension between attention and distraction as a frame for sinfulness and redemption. In so far as we are distracted, we slide away from God's love; we lose ourselves – ultimately kill ourselves – in any number of tempting sins. For example, David Marno, whose study of Donne's poetry inspired the title of this volume, argues that this tension is at the heart of John Donne's devotional poetry. In his book *Death Be Not Proud*,[4] he explores how Donne worked sonnets to take us from distraction to attention, from sinfulness to redemption.

Donne uses the structure and language of the poem to gather the attention of the reader. When we are engaged in faithful prayer, we receive God's grace with thankfulness for the gift of redemption. Instead of the distractions of *sarx* – the body with its cravings and appetites – the poem enables a human, incarnate attention to grow in a grace that incorporates distraction, just as God took on the frailties and death of human flesh in Christ. As we arrive at the end of the poem, we are able to assert 'Death, thou shalt die!' – and as we do so, we affirm the reality of the resurrection. Eternal life is ours, here and now. The knowledge that results from reading one of Donne's holy sonnets is the knowledge of holy attention. As we attend to the sonnet, our attention becomes holy, and we grow more deeply into the knowledge of faith, transformed to become more Christ-like.

Simone Weil describes the same process when she encountered George Herbert's poem 'Love':

> [a young English Catholic] told me of the existence of those English poets of the 17C who are named metaphysical. In reading them later on, I discovered the poem … called Love. I learnt it by heart. Often, at the culminating point of a violent headache, I make myself say it over, concentrating all my attention upon it and clinging with all my soul to the tenderness it enshrines.

4 David Marno, *Death Be Not Proud: The Art of Holy Attention* (Chicago, IL: Chicago University Press, 2016).

> I used to think I was merely reciting it as a beautiful poem, but without my knowing it the recitation had the virtue of a prayer. It was during one of these recitations that, as I told you, Christ himself came down and took possession of me.[5]

The resources are there, within our Christian tradition, to enable a holy attention that transforms. Those resources are prayers or biblical passages, creeds, psalms, or hymns known off by heart, or particular art that enables us to gaze with a holy attention, or poetry. Or music. All like icons that capture and shape our attention towards God.

The ability to gather attention becomes, as Williams and Crawford suggest, a political and moral imperative in a world that now turns on an attention economy. How can those traditional practices of our Christian heritage enable humanity to find itself in its ability to ignore distraction and attend to God?

One way is to celebrate the craft of preaching. Preaching commands attention at the heart of worship. With phones switched off, and the intention to worship God, the sermon can gather those present into a greater awareness of God's grace transforming their lives. Those who preach have a God-given opportunity to enable listeners to encounter Jesus Christ, away from the distraction of wandering thought and restless sense.

The sermon offers something different from the clickbait that commodifies the attention and seduces human intention, the very self, in today's market economy. It gives the opportunity to gaze on the living Christ, crucified and risen, and attend to the transformative power of the love of God as individuals in the Church and the world. God claims the attention as the preacher enables the contemplation of the promise of eternal, abundant life, instead of becoming distracted and dissipated in a shallow morass of trivial and false gratifications.

---

5 Simone Weil, *Waiting on God: The Essence of her Thought*, translated from the French by Emma Craufurd (Glasgow: Collins, Fount Paperbacks, [1951] 1977), p. 35.

As the person encounters Christ, they are transformed. The impact isn't just individual. The whole of society is involved. James Williams writes, after he realized what the impact of the digital economy was:

> I knew this wasn't just about *me* – my deep distractions, my frustrated goals. But when most people in society use your product, you aren't just designing users; you're designing society. But if all of society were to become as distracted in this new, deep way as I was starting to feel, what would that mean? What would be the implications for our shared interests, our common purposes, our collective identities, our politics?[6]

The broader consequences for society of a human attention that is commodified to distraction, are becoming apparent. Williams warns that '[F]uture generations will judge us not only for our stewardship of the outer environment, but of the inner environment as well.' [7]

The word, heard and preached, should hopefully stir a response of thanksgiving, an awareness of the deeper reality of God's gifts, including the sacrament of Christ's Body and Blood. Together, via word and sacrament, the worshipper becomes a member of a body that is caught up into God's grace and able to withstand the forces and pressures that fragment and atomize the human self today.

This collection is offered to inspire preachers to engage with the craft of writing and delivering sermons, as part of worship that captures the attention. This is to understand how fragments are gathered, like grain once scattered in the fields and grapes once dispersed on the hillside. It is to pray that ancient prayer that the whole Church be gathered from the corners of the earth into God's Kingdom. It is to show a way for fragmented selves to find wholeness instead of all that distracts us in life.

---

6 Williams, *Stand Out of Our Light*, p. 10.
7 Williams, *Stand Out of Our Light*, p. 127.

The Church gathers the fragments as morsels collected into 12 baskets after the feeding of the 5,000. For though we are many, we are one body, sharing the one bread. It is to be reminded of the profound reality that humanity finds its fulfilment in the wholeness of God. As we attend to God, we find our place within God's desires and purposes for us to be together in Christ's presence.

This book offers rich reflections on the joy of responding to the vocation to preach. It's a vocation that has borne fruit throughout the ages and, with renewed vigour and purpose, now has much to contribute to a distracted world, where it is all too difficult to gather attention, individually or corporately.

The chapters explore how preaching begins in attention – attention to God, the author of all; to Christ, who is the living Word, the Alpha and Omega; to the Holy Spirit, who inspires and makes bold the disciple to tell of their faith.

As the tradition of devotion reminds us, our thinking and sermon preparation begins by asking for God's grace, in thankfulness for the gifts and givens of life and ministry. As Marno comments of Donne's poetry, 'the poetry of attention becomes an instrument of asking and thanking for divine grace.'[8] A sermon begins in the same movement. It is by thanking that we think.[9]

Edmund Newey describes how the encounter with Scripture is full of life '... like an encounter with a scarcely containable power, almost akin to Jacob wrestling with the angel at Peniel'. He says the process that ends at the preached word is 'increasingly like an encounter with the mystery of God's self-communication that has the quality of a sacrament, if not quite a theophany'. The processes of preparation begin in prayer and often in struggle. The preacher then turns to the Scriptures that bear witness to God; to the people whose lives God has touched

8 Marno, *Death Be Not Proud*, p. 214.
9 Marno, *Death Be Not Proud*, p. 27.

and whose response God invites; to the occasion, the time and place, on which the sermon is being offered, and finally again to God, in whose embrace this attentiveness is held.

Richard Sudworth has ministered and preached all his life in parishes that have been dominated by other faith communities. He attends, in his chapter, to the texts that are in danger of becoming strange to us, and asks how, as a Christian, the preacher might engage, ethically and honourably, with 'the Jewishness of so much of our Scriptures and the tradition that provides inextricable roots to the Church'

Joel Love attends to the Holy Spirit, as he takes us to the experience of Pentecost, and what it means to preach 'each in our own language.' He reflects on St Peter's sermon on the day of Pentecost (Acts 2), a sermon about the Holy Spirit that is explicitly empowered by the Spirit. Love elucidates how homiletics, the art of preaching, is a branch of pneumatology as it includes the business of interpreting and translating:

> It is the Spirit of God who bears witness to Christ, who takes what is hidden and reveals it to us, and who enables us to communicate the gospel in a variety of voices and contexts … Faithful improvisation 'in the Spirit' can take place in the library or in the preacher's study as well as in Lectio Divina, prayer meetings, and Bible studies. The key is that God's Spirit be involved both in the preparation and in the proclamation of the word.'

Jessica Martin reminds us that preaching captures the attention in particular times and places. The eloquence of Lancelot Andrewes echoes and reverberates through a sermon preached at his death, and onwards, a living word that begins with those present, around his dead body. The word of the sermon is preached and takes life as an embodied performance.

Sr Judith SLG is a member of an enclosed religious order. Her chapter offers a personal account of her engagement with Lectio Divina, which is a particular way of attending to the word of

God. Silence is at the heart of this encounter. This is to cultivate the discipline of attention, drawing on traditions of meditation and contemplation that are alive within the religious life. The focus is on listening, receiving, openness to what comes from the grace of God.

Attention to the Other in Lectio Divina is to the word of God as read or heard in Scripture. Preaching requires attention to the others around us as well. It is not, as sometimes thought, words delivered six feet above contradiction, but an engagement, a conversation, with others, attending to what is said by those with whom we relate. Victoria Johnson explains how the word ὁμιλεῖν, from which we get the word 'homily', means to dialogue or converse. She refers to the story in Luke's Gospel, where the disciples, on the road to Emmaus, were talking and discussing, when Jesus himself came near and walked with them. Their lives were changed for ever by this sermon that was a conversation that brought about conversion of life. At its heart, within the conversation or dialogue that is the sermon, there will be a call to be changed or converted, and a call to action.

Anderson Jeremiah graphically describes his own experience of conversion, as he preached to a congregation in India, and was changed for ever. He attends to the subaltern presence and voices of those with whom he ministers, wondering about the power relation between the preacher and the congregation where he lives in Lancaster, in the north of England. How can the preacher, and the Church in which sermons happen, engage better with those who struggle within a matrix of poverty and exclusion? He argues that 'sermons and preaching, as a means of our faith, need to show real sensitivity to those who share the experience of breaking open the word of God; preaching must connect with the lived realities of people. The challenge is to see how the voices of those who are silenced, ignored and marginalized within the Church can be embraced and articulated. Then the Church should engage critically with the social and political matrix that determines the context.'

Preaching, as conversation, needs to be attentive to the needs and perspectives of those whose voices are not normally heard. In a UK that is bitterly divided after the Referendum of 2016, Jeremiah's chapter needs to be heard and taken to heart.

Rachel Mann attends to her own body as she preaches at a 'Christians at Pride' festival occasion at St James' Church, Piccadilly in July 2017. How does one prepare for such an occasion? What does your body feel and experience? How do you attend to the particularities of place and time, weather, crowds, delays, dehydration? The terror and joy that you feel? She found herself taking off her sandals to preach barefoot, in the nave, in that crowded church. She spoke of hope and the surprise of grace, of trauma and exclusion. She spoke of how the Church has changed and how it has not changed, for both good and ill. She spoke of Jesus Christ, into the experience of being LGBT*[10] in today's world.

Frances Ward describes a funeral she took of a popular teenager who died of leukaemia. How does one try to capture the unspeakability of such an occasion to a church full of school friends and family, who are face to face with the incomprehensible death of someone full of promise and life? How does the preacher hold the attention, and seek to transform the grief of a congregation that no longer has much idea of Christianity? Where traditional words break down? What is it to try and speak of a reality that undergirds human existence and is never exhausted? Where our words reach their limit, and stretch towards the incarnate Word that is Jesus Christ? She wonders about what it means to be human, and face loss and grief, as she contemplates the stone memorials that were carved in town centres after World War One. What does it mean to say *Ecce Homo*, not as Nietzsche did, as he affirmed the eternal recurrence of Man, but as our words find their place and open us to an encounter with the living Word of Jesus Christ,

10 Lesbian, Gay, Bisexual and Transgender. The * signifies further spectrums of sexuality and gender.

revealing the love of God, in whom we are held and enabled to grow and flourish eternally?

This is not a 'how-to' book. It doesn't give step-by-step techniques and tips. It trusts the preacher today to want to engage seriously and wholeheartedly with the joy and terror of thinking through and delivering a sermon – whether scripted, or *ex tempore*. Often the contributors offer an anecdote, or situation, that prompted them to struggle with God's presence and meaning, struggling for the blessing that they hoped would emerge. They have tried to remain true to the cost of preaching the word of God; how more often than not it takes them towards the cross, to witness to the crucified Christ before the life-giving power of the resurrection became a blessing. Even then, it is never the invitation to rest in complacency, but always to accept a further challenge, to live a fuller restlessness, either as preacher, or as listener, in whom the word of God is brought to greater life.

Because the word that is preached is an embodied word, an incarnate word, the preacher's own presence in the midst of a congregation or gathering of those willing to listen is important. So is the way the preached word belongs within the body of Christ, calling that body always to transcend itself into Christ; always restless for the Kingdom of God, ever watchful for the times when it draws near.

The preacher attends to the congregation, to what will enable them to listen and hear the Word of God, the living Christ, crucified and risen in their company. She will seek to be aware of how persons can be fearful and, in their fear, be contemptuous of others. The word 'congregation' means to gather together; so the preacher enables the gathering of attention among all those involved, drawing attention to the Scriptures, seeking the ways in which they interpreted the living Christ, crucified and risen, in their own time and place. The preacher will attend to the world, alive with the promise of God yet troubled by injustice, terror, violence.

The chapters are interspersed with sermons that follow

through the Church year, from Advent to All Saints. These are not served as illustrations, but as a variety of offerings that show a range of ways in which the preacher, inspired with an open attention to God, to the living Christ, crucified and risen, to the world around, can offer lively sermons to enable the person, the Church and the world to attend to what really matters and be energized by the Holy Spirit.

Paula Gooder contributes an Afterword, as she commends the place of the sermon in today's Church and world. Preachers seek to communicate their conviction that the word of God is vital and generative, deserving of our attention in this age, as in all ages, past and future. All the contributors hope that this volume will encourage preachers today into boldness and confidence, into skill and expertise, into a real and open dependence on the grace of God.

In many pulpits, the words from John 12.21 can be seen – a stark reminder to the preacher already mindful of the enormity of the task in which they are engaged: 'We would see Jesus'. In an age where our attention is scarce and claims upon it are hotly contested and where our humanity is shaped by what we attend to, this book seeks to encourage and enable the preacher to witness to the living Christ, crucified and risen, in ways that are transformative of the self, Church and world.

1

Exacting Attention: Preaching as Witness

EDMUND NEWEY

The best sermons are exacting: in composition, delivery and reception alike they require attention. To make this claim is not to diminish the many other forms of address that are needed in Christian ministry. An all-age talk, an *ex tempore* homily at a care home, a guided meditation, a school assembly – each has a different geometry and requires other qualities, but in my experience the more *attentive* a formal sermon is, the better it will be. The difficulty lies in establishing what this quality of attention is about. It need not mean difficulty, length or erudition. It does, however, have something to do with seriousness – a demand placed on both the preacher and the congregation to heed the word of God, present in the readings, present in the practices of the Christian community being spoken to, and above all present in the risen Christ to whom they both point. It also has to do with context, a sensitivity to time and place that is very obvious when it is lacking. In principle, I have no problem with preaching a sermon more than once, but it is interesting to observe how 're-deployed' sermons succeed or fail. In my experience, they fail if they have simply been lifted from the drawer, because they lack a proper context in the current life and concerns of the preacher and a congruence with the needs of the listening community; they can succeed if they are owned anew. A good sermon, then, is a call to attend – to God, self, neighbours and world. Aesthetically it may be a very long way from a well-formed poem or work of art, but in common with them it offers an invitation to step aside that frees speaker and hearer alike to see afresh.

This chapter begins with Cranmer's Collect for the Second Sunday in Advent, also used as the Collect for Bible Sunday. The sharply focused lens of this prayer helps us to see more clearly the scope of what is asked of us in preaching the word of God. I then turn to the effect of such preaching. The preacher's purpose cannot be merely to *communicate* a message – every preacher knows the risk and the ambiguity of a sermon, how differently its meaning may be heard by different people – so the sermon is better seen as an act of witness, spoken by and addressed to people 'who do not yet exist'.[11] Preaching, in other words, is an exercise in *prolepsis*, reaching out to the Kingdom of God that is both now and not yet. Finally, I look at a recent sermon by Trevor Mwamba as a model of this attentive witness, before concluding that it is with the summons '*Ecce Homo*' that preaching ultimately presents us.

Wrestling with the word

> Blessed Lord, who hast caused all holy Scriptures to be written for our learning; grant that we may in such wise hear them, read, mark, learn, and inwardly digest them, that by patience, and comfort of thy holy Word, we may embrace, and ever hold fast the blessed hope of everlasting life, which thou hast given us in our Saviour Jesus Christ. Amen.[12]

The Collect for the Second Sunday in Advent is one of a small number of new compositions, most of them generally accepted to be by Cranmer, for the 1549 Book of Common Prayer. Even now its five famous verbs – hear, read, mark, learn and digest – are deeply engrained in the fabric of Anglican worship,

---

11 Rowan Williams, *Holy Living* (London: Bloomsbury, 2017), p. 97, condensing the argument of Jacob Needleman in *Lost Christianity* (New York: Penguin, 2003).

12 The Book of Common Prayer, Collect for the Second Sunday of Advent.

summoning us to a seriousness in our approach to the Bible that is characteristically Protestant. But the blessing of those five modes of active engagement with the Scriptures is framed by the prayer in a wider context. The individual's encounter with particular texts is set within the compass of the Bible as a whole, within the lifelong journey of 'learning', and finally within the eschatological embrace of 'the blessed hope of everlasting life'. The 'comfort of thy holy Word' here is as much the incarnate Word of Christ as the written word of Scripture. The serious encounter with the Scriptures is thus sacramental in character: an encounter with Christ himself.

In recent years, I have found my own attempts to preach the word increasingly faced with this sacramental challenge. In my early years as a preacher I tended to think of the sermon as an opportunity to engage with the set readings rather as I had done in my undergraduate studies of literature: here were texts of richness and depth, whose dimensions it was my task to elucidate. More recently, both in reading Scripture – in public and private – and in preaching on it, the engagement has felt much more like an encounter with a scarcely containable power, almost akin to Jacob wrestling with the angel at Peniel. I am not sure how different the result is, but the process by which I arrive at the preached word now seems increasingly like an encounter with the mystery of God's self-communication that has the quality of a sacrament, if not quite a theophany.

In his book *Hand to Hand: Listening to the Work of Art*, Jean-Louis Chrétien characterizes the artistic process as a 'wrestling with the irresistible'. He cites Rainer Maria Rilke's poem 'Der Schauende', alluding to Jacob and his struggle with the angel (Genesis 32.22–31):

Whomever this Angel overcame
(who so often declined the fight),
he walks erect and justified
and great out of that hard hand
which, as if sculpting, nestled round him.

Winning does not tempt him.
His growth is: to be the deeply defeated
by ever greater things.[13]

Jacob struggles with the angel, emerging wounded but victorious, yet not in any conventional sense: 'deeply defeated / by ever greater things'. Jacob's re-naming as 'Israel' at the end of the struggle is the mark of a victory-in-defeat and defeat-in-victory in which he sees, touches, tastes, hears and smells the living one, but never learns his name. Our hearing, reading, marking, learning and inward digesting of the word has just the same character, leading us into the sacramental embrace of God in Christ.

It is attention of this sort – all-consuming, transformative, yet never complete – that a sermon requires at every stage, from its preparation to its delivery and then its reception by the congregation, attention being paid:

- to God in *prayer*
- to the *Scriptures* that bear witness to God
- to the *people* whose lives God has touched and whose response God invites
- to the occasion, the *time and place*, on which the sermon is being offered
- and finally again to *God*, in whose embrace this attentiveness is held.

Each of these moments or facets of attention inhabits, at least potentially, the same time and space of human-divine encounter as the theophany at Peniel.

Preaching begins in *prayer*. This imperative is succinctly summarized by Augustine in a passage from *On Christian Teaching* in which he requires that the preacher be 'a person of prayer before a person of words (*orator antequam dictor*)':

13 Jean-Louis Chrétien, *Hand to Hand: Listening to the Work of Art* (New York: Fordham, 2003), p. 2; citing Rainer Maria Rilke, *Die Gedichte* (Frankfurt: Insel, 2006), p. 346.

> [The preacher] should be in no doubt that any ability he has ... derives more from his devotion to prayer than his dedication to oratory; and so, by praying for himself and those he is about to address, he must become a man of prayer before a man of words. As the hour of his address approaches, before he opens his thrusting lips he should lift his thirsting soul to God so that he may utter what he has drunk in and pour out what has filled him.[14]

Augustine's focus here, though primarily on prayer immediately prior to the act of preaching, is also on the need for prayer to be part of the consistent character of the preacher. As he puts it later in the same work, 'people do not listen with obedience to the man who does not listen to himself [i.e. does not heed his own lessons]'.[15] Nonetheless, to adapt the Thirty-Nine Articles of Religion, 'the unworthiness of the minister hindereth not the efficacy' of the sermon, because it is finally not to the preacher but to Christ that the hearers are listening. Citing Paul, Augustine is clear that Christ may be shown forth even by those who fail to adhere to his teaching – 'Let Christ be proclaimed, whether in pretence or in truth' (Philippians 1.18) – but he will more readily find fertile ground when there is consonance between word and deed in the one who preaches it.

Next it is essential that preaching be rooted in studious and careful reading, above all, of the *Scriptures*. The call here is to dwell in the word, avoiding both the biblicist temptation to treat Scripture as 'an inspired supernatural guide for individual conduct' and the liberal tendency to see it as 'a piece of detached historical record'. The proper stance towards the Bible is neither slavish submission nor detached mastery, but simply reverent attention. As Rowan Williams puts it:

> Before Scripture is read in private it is heard in public ... Very few

14 Augustine, *On Christian Teaching* (Oxford: Oxford University Press, 1997), 4, XIV, p. 121.

15 Augustine, *On Christian Teaching*, 4, XXVII, p. 143.

> early or mediaeval Christians could possibly have owned a Bible; not many in the rapidly growing churches of the developing world today are likely to either. And this underlines the fact that the Church's public use of the Bible represents the Church as defined in some important way by listening ... It silences itself to hear something, representing itself in that moment as a community existing in response to a word of summons or invitation, to an act of communication that requires to be heard and answered.[16]

Third, keen attention to the *people* of God who will hear the sermon is called for. This attention is primarily pastoral and, like the preacher's attentiveness in prayer and to Scripture, asks for the ability to place oneself alongside those addressed, understanding the context from which they are encountering the preached word. In my current cathedral setting the sheer variety of worshippers and the relative impermanence of my relationship with many of them makes this more of a challenge than in a parish. Yet my experience of cathedral life is that one's understanding, though narrow, may be surprisingly deep. One of the great privileges of serving in a choral foundation is the frequency with which people find themselves opened up spiritually by the worship. Faces, care-worn on entering the church, are transformed as they leave – and sometimes those faces belong to people who have a profound desire to convey something of what has touched them spiritually, an unburdening eased by their anonymity and the fact that they may not be here again. And if this is the journey made by the congregation it is also one made by the clergy and ministers, as the relatively low demands for active participation free them to share in, rather than lead, worship. In *Lost Christianity*, Jacob Needleman locates the value of contemplative practices not so much in the experience of God that they might furnish, but simply 'in the experience of existing as such';[17] or, as Rowan Williams puts it when speaking of Saint Benedict: 'The product of the workshop

16 Williams, *Holy Living*, pp. 31, 45.

17 Jacob Needleman in *Lost Christianity* (New York: Penguin, 2003), p. 117.

[of the Christian community] is people who are *really there*.'[18] This, then, is the goal of the attention paid to the community addressed by the preacher, of which he or she is also a part: to learn the true nature of one's own existence and that of those alongside whom one works.

The character of this levelling out of the difference between givers and receivers of ministry is again captured beautifully by Augustine:

> In virtue of the duty assigned to us we guard you, brothers and sisters, but our desire is to be guarded by God along with you. We act as your shepherds, but we along with you are sheep under the one shepherd. We stand in this elevated position as your instructors, but we are your fellow-students in this school under our one teacher.[19]

Or, as he puts it elsewhere:

> Listen to me; nay, rather, listen *with* me. Let us listen together; let us learn together. For the fact that I am speaking and you are listening does not mean that I am not listening along with you. For, in this school we are all fellow students; heaven is the chair of our professor.[20]

Fourth, the preacher must attend to the particularity of the *time and place* in which the sermon is offered. Here the need is to locate oneself at the incarnational intersection between a *patient* attention to time and place – the horizontal axis – and an *urgent* attention to the vertical axis of redemption. The different senses of time known as *kronos* and *kairos* are brought together in the sermon which must seek to expound God's word here and now, but also acknowledge the placing of the here and now in the great narrative of God's grace.

---

18 Williams, *Holy Living*, p. 64 (emphasis added).

19 Augustine, *Expositions of the Psalms*, vol. 6 (New York: New City Press, 2004), Psalm 126, p. 86.

20 Augustine, *Sermons on the Liturgical Seasons* (Washington: Catholic University of America Press, p. 380), Sermon 261.

And finally, the preacher must return to *God*, whose abiding is the foundation on which all these various forms of attention are built. As Jean-Louis Chrétien writes, 'the highest attention loses itself in what it attends to':[21] there is a deliberate filtering out of the distraction of Martha's 'many things' for the sake of Mary's 'one thing' (Luke 10.38–42). But when the one thing attended to is the one who holds all that is in being, the attention is freed to new levels of generosity, re-making God's people as human beings constituted by an alertness to God's presence in all times and places. This, of course, is a condition shaped more by hope than by actuality – these are people, to cite Needleman again, 'who do not yet exist'– but their existence is one that preachers are called to glimpse, imagine and aspire to for themselves and the communities we serve.

In rehearsing each of these five facets of attention it will be evident that at each stage there is a call to participation, to see human nature caught up in the embrace of divine grace (2 Peter 1.4). *Prayer*, by its very nature, is a sharing in the Spirit, in George Herbert's phrase, 'God's breath in man returning to his birth'.[22] The *Scriptures*, like the incarnate Word to whom they bear witness, are:

> At one and the same time human and divine: not divine on the one hand and human on the other, divine here and human there and especially not divine where it suits me and human where it doesn't, but entirely human and entirely divine.[23]

The *people* one is with is the only community where the godly life can be made real, and the preached attention to particular people in a particular *time and place*, like the liturgy itself, anticipates the Kingdom of God, where holiness is not a flight into abstraction

21 Jean-Louis Chrétien, *Pour reprendre et perdre haleine: Dix brèves méditations* (Paris: Bayard, 2009), p. 71.

22 George Herbert, 'Prayer (1)', *The Complete English Poems* (Harmondsworth: Penguin, 1991), p. 45.

23 Jean-Louis Chrétien, *Sous le regard de la Bible* (Paris: Bayard, 2008), p. 17.

but simply 'an unselfconscious getting-used-to-others', knowing their needs.[24]

All of this may seem to place an unbearable burden on the preacher, but this need not be so if we bear in mind that the call is to show Christ, in Aquinas' phrase about God, *totum, sed non totaliter*[25] – as a whole, not in his entirety. Adapting St Thomas's words to a new context in evangelism that applies equally to the witness of preaching, Chrétien says this:

> The witness to Christ shows the whole Christ, but does not show him completely and comprehensively; the witness does not exhaust the truth of the one to whom she bears witness. In her testimony space is left for other witnesses, whose face and voice and life and doings will in their turn bear a faithful witness that is whole but not complete.[26]

Becoming witnesses

The best-known of the diagnoses of the Myers-Briggs Type Indicator, familiar to most Anglican clergy of recent generations, is the separation of personalities into the Jungian categories of extravert and introvert, the former being those who gain energy from being with others, the latter being those who do so by being alone. For all its value in helping us to understand the variety of human personality types, I am not convinced that the extravert/introvert distinction works well for the act of preaching. Good preaching, in my experience, is a re-energizing activity for hearer and speaker alike, wherever they are on the extraversion/introversion spectrum; and, conversely, bad preaching is draining for both preacher and congregation. Again, in the words of Jean-Louis Chrétien, 'in speaking to others one is not discharging previously accumulated energy, one continues to acquire new

24 Williams, *Holy Living*, p. 55.

25 *Summa Theologiae*, Ia, 12, 7.

26 Chrétien, *Sous le regard de la Bible*, p. 133.

energy even as one expends it'.[27] Chrétien does not have sermons specifically in mind here, but his words are apt for the experience of preaching. Sermons that are attentively prepared, delivered and received have an ability to nourish that is, once again, sacramental in character.

A sharper way of expressing this is to say that sermons given and received as acts of witness will energize preacher and congregation alike; sermons that duck this challenge will distract and drain. An example may help here: an instance of the preacher's common experience of being heard to say something quite different from what was intended.

Preaching recently as a guest in a local parish on the feast of Christ the King, I set out two scriptural perspectives on Christ's kingship: the heavenly kingship witnessed to in Revelation and the very different earthly kingship seen in John's account of his trial and crucifixion, both being encounters with the truth of Christ – triumphant in the first case; bound, imprisoned and defenceless in the second – then drawing the conclusion that our earthly witness to Jesus' lordship is set between these two poles. At the door afterwards a good number thanked me for my words, but even as they did so I could sense the approach of a listener whose reaction had been very different. Waiting until I was free, she politely began by thanking me for coming, before expressing her dismay at what I had said. One way of characterizing her case against the sermon would be to call it a difference of theological perspective: hers seeing the kingship of Christ as a reality in which his followers share fully, to be proclaimed fearlessly in the world; mine perceiving it as a truth unequivocally revealed, but as yet only partially apprehended, even within the Church. Here, one might say, was a classic case of theological disagreement and it was certainly in those terms that I improvised a response.

But to describe this as a theological disagreement is partly to misrepresent it: it was, I think, more fundamental than that. This

27 Jean-Louis Chrétien, *Sous le regard de la Bible*, p. 72.

was a case of inattention: on the listener's part by hearing what was preached through the filter of a set of expectations about what should be said on such a theme; on my part by not taking sufficiently seriously the centrality of the lordship of Christ to the faith of a largely evangelical congregation. At the root of both, failures of attention are the same problem: the Church, like social media, can easily become an echo chamber where one's own theological reference points are taken as normative. I have more than once caught myself reacting to 'unsound' sermons with similar depth of feeling: looking for certain boxes to be ticked and, when they are not, spending the rest of the sermon formulating my disagreements, rather than attending to what is being said.[28] I clearly recall a sermon that enraged me in my early twenties. Quoting (out of context, to my mind) Johnny Cash's line 'you're so heavenly minded you're no earthly good', the preacher made the case that church worship is only a minor part of Christianity, and that it's what happens outside that matters. As a struggling newly qualified teacher this was not what I wanted to hear: church for me was an indispensable island of solace in the midst of an ocean of stress. So off I went on one of my ranting interior monologues: it's all very well clergy going on about the dangers of church; maybe they've had enough of it, but I certainly haven't …

The deeper point here is that preaching is not simply about communicating a message: it is an act of witness. The increasing prevalence of the language of 'communication' in contemporary culture encourages us to see human interaction in terms of transferring sets of information, whether facts or opinions, from those who have them to those who don't. Yet every preacher knows that sermons very rarely pass on information unambiguously: nuggets of wisdom of which the preacher is so proud are barely noticed; throw-away remarks are taken as gospel; sometimes, it seems, almost the opposite

28 C. S. Lewis has wise insights on this temptation in *The Screwtape Letters* (London: Collins, 2012), chapter 16.

meaning from the one intended is what is heard. The advantage of this ambiguity is that the grace of God has scope to be at work, and it will be all the more freely present if the sermon is understood not as an attempt at communication, but primarily as testimony.

To see the sermon as an act of witness is to place it in its proper context as a unique episode in the unfolding story of God's purposes for the world. The fivefold attention outline above – to God in *prayer*, to the *Scriptures*, to the *people* being addressed, to the *time and place*, and again to *God*, in whose embrace this attentiveness is held – is, like worship in general, a gathering before God (*coram Deo*) that is at the same time before God's people (*coram hominibus*). And the sermon bears witness to this context: here God's people are gathered around God's word, to be re-made in the service of God's world. One of the central manifestations of this re-making is the sermon as an act of testimony, for 'it is the testimony that makes the witness, not the witness who makes the testimony ...'[29] The test, then, is not the sincerity, 'soundness' or relevance of the preacher and her words, but simply the degree to which what is said and the way it is said and heard bear witness to God, opening the lives of those present to the life of the living one.

Trevor Mwamba

Can this high calling ever be lived up to? It is a difficult, exacting vocation; but I suspect that every churchgoer has a short list of transformative sermons, heard and read, that would meet the criteria. The list will be different for everyone because, as Chrétien acknowledges, each witness is irreplaceable. Citing examples is fraught with danger, especially when the sermons being quoted are written records of the spoken word. Nonetheless, one recent volume that seems to me to best reflect this spirit of attentiveness

29 Chrétien, *Sous le regard de la Bible*, pp. 121, 129.

and to speak to a wide spectrum of readers is Trevor Mwamba's *Dancing Sermons.*

These addresses, delivered in a variety of contexts from Oxford colleges to the Bishop's own Cathedral of the Holy Cross in Gaborone, Botswana, are notable for their unassuming simplicity of structure and delivery. Often they begin with a succinct opening remark that doesn't so much summarize what is to come as act as a call to attention: the paragraphs are frequently only a short sentence in length and drop down the page rather like the blocks of text in a modernist poem; they are not conventionally sequential, yet they combine to form a coherent arc leading the reader or listener into the 'strange new world of the Bible' and the God to whom it points. Mwamba's sermons do not conform to most canons of homiletic best practice, yet as acts of witness they are unquestionably compelling.

The highlight of the collection for me is a sermon, preached on Ash Wednesday 1998 in Keble College Chapel, Oxford, on the homeless gospel passage commonly printed as John 8.1–11. It begins with a short sentence: 'A woman is caught in the act of adultery, but what about the Man?'[30] The arresting question opens up a host of stimulating lines of thought about this enigmatic passage, but most importantly it points us straight away to the status of this episode as an act of revelation, a theophany in which the nature of God is manifested: 'what about the Man?', the capitals indicating that here we are dealing with the Man who is one with God. This potentially portentous opening is immediately undercut by the second and third paragraphs that are as homely as they come:

> Lent begins this week. As we begin our Lenten observance, I would like to offer you a thought or two on how we cultivate our spiritual life.
>
> Most of us think of Lent as a time of self-denial, when for example

30 Trevor Mwamba, *Dancing Sermons* (Edinburgh: Maclean Dubois, 2006), pp. 24f.

> we stop chewing gum, give up chocolate, or stop watching *Neighbours* on TV.

The sermon proceeds by the close juxtaposition of these two registers: theological depth and the challenge of the gospel on the one hand; the approachable and the familiar on the other. So we have the amusing description of an episode in the life of Truro Cathedral on a hot summer Sunday, where the Canon Chancellor and his colleagues are caught on the hop trying to decide what to do about a member of the congregation – a young woman, undeniably pious but also scarcely clad – the outcome of which is that:

> In true Anglican fashion, they unanimously decided to do nothing at all. Let her alone and hope for the best.

This apparently light-hearted anecdote, told with gentle humour, imperceptibly becomes the occasion for a meditation on the nakedness of the human condition before God: our nakedness is not a cause for shame, but for rejoicing, as in it we share in Christ's condition on the cross, naked, 'as nature formed us, God being our Creator'.

Mwamba then offers a summary of the forms of dress we put on to hide our nakedness: 'We all dress up in some bright or dark garment of sorts. And in it we all hide ourselves from what we really are and what God can do for us':

> The dress of status
> The dress of learning
> The dress of power
> The dress of race
> The dress of self-righteousness
> The dress of pride
> The dress of self-sufficiency. I am all right, Jack. I don't know about you.
> We also dress up in the negative. The dress of low self-esteem.

The dress of shame
The dress of emptiness
The dress of humiliation
The dress of failure
The dress of disappointments, and shattered dreams.

This list, compact and compendious at once, forms a picture poem on the page, its silhouette both that of a human being and gesturing to the cross; and this graphic image is followed immediately by the experience of the woman: 'The offence: adultery. Very serious indeed, they had it all on video.' Suddenly the irrefutable truth, both of the woman's offence and of the human capacity for hiding the truth about ourselves, are revealed to be as nothing, as light as a feather, when they are brought into the presence of Christ.

There is an old spiritual song that goes, 'There is a place of quiet rest where sin cannot molest. It's close to the heart of God.' So the woman caught in adultery found a place of 'quiet rest where sin cannot molest', being close to Jesus, the friend of sinners …

There is a place where sin cannot molest. It is in the presence of Christ. In this presence, just as we are, we should in the period of Lent be transformed to be better people. Learn not to condemn others hastily, learn to see our failings, learn of the forgiving love of God for us, learn ultimately to be like Jesus who offers this gift.

And so the sermon ends: less than 1,000 words encapsulating the Lenten lesson of God's abundant mercy; a profound testimony delivered gently and humorously.

Conclusion

Mwamba's sermon is a beautiful example of what we might call exegesis as participation, paying very close attention to the biblical text but doing so in a way that, because it also pays attention to God, to the hearers and to the context, draws us closely into the embrace of the one to whom it bears witness. This exacting attention gives the sermon a sacramental form, opening it to the Holy Spirit, without whose interpreting the word will not be made known. As Jeremy Taylor puts it in a sermon entitled '*Via intelligentiae*' ('the way of understanding'):

> For although the scriptures themselves are written by the Spirit of God, yet they are written within and without: and besides the light that shines upon the face of them, unless there be a light shining within our hearts, unfolding the leaves, and interpreting the mysterious sense of the Spirit, convincing our consciences and preaching to our hearts, to look for Christ in the leaves of the gospel, is to look for the living amongst the dead. There is life in them, but that life is, according to St Paul's expression, 'hid with Christ in God'; and unless the Spirit of God be the *promo-condus*, we shall never draw it forth.[31]

Every sermon is an opportunity for preacher and congregation alike to 'be surprising / A hunger in himself to be more serious',[32] to be drawn by this unique act of witness and 'launched on a process of interwoven divine gift and human exploration'.[33] It is sometimes said that a sermon should be preached as much *from* conversion as *for* conversion and this, I think, is at the root of preaching as witness. Engaging seriously in this task, the preacher is heeding the instruction of the letter of James:

> But be doers of the word, and not merely hearers who deceive themselves. For if any are hearers of the word and not doers, they are like those who look at themselves* in a mirror; for they look at themselves and, on going away, immediately forget what they were like. But those who look into the perfect law, the law of liberty, and persevere, being not hearers who forget but doers

31 Jeremy Taylor, *Selected Works* (New York: Paulist Press, 1990), p. 374.

32 Philip Larkin, 'Church-going', *The Complete Poems* (London: Faber & Faber, 2012), p. 36.

33 Williams, *Holy Living*, p. 169.

who act–they will be blessed in their doing. (James 1.22–25)

The usual translation 'be doers of the word … not hearers …' misses the force of the original, which as Karl Barth observes was made explicit by Calvin's rendering: 'be doers of the word and not merely listeners'.[34] The imperative is to be *poietai logou*, those who actively do what the Word Incarnate does, whom to serve is perfect freedom, rather than passively listening to him.

The low conception of preaching into which it is so easy to slip treats the sermon as an interlude in an act of worship when we may listen to something that makes the Scriptures relevant, hopefully with a touch of humour on the way. The high calling is to know that the sermon is a time of encounter with God. The purpose of the sermon thus understood is that preacher and congregation alike should be brought to the place where they can hear Nathan's words to David, 'You are the man!' (2 Samuel 12.7) and Pilate's words to the condemned Christ 'Here is the Man!' (John 19.5). Both these versions of *Ecce Homo* are the goal of the sermon, which should *both* convict us of our failure *and* place us in the presence of the one who alone sets us free from that failure, so that we may testify that truly the Lord is in this place – in us: here, now.

34 Karl Barth, *Church Dogmatics* (London: T&T Clark, 2002), 1, ii, section 18, pp. 365–7.

A Sermon for Advent: Encountering the Dangerous God

RACHEL MANN

God can be most curious. He has a gift for calling the oddest, most unexpected people into his service. Indeed, one might almost claim that oddness and curiousness are basic requirements among the called. Consider Moses, the coward who runs away from the scene of a murder. He runs and, in the presence of the fire of God, insists on his unsuitability as a leader and is finally sent back to bring God's people out of slavery. Or Jonah whose primary gift is – it would seem – to just run and keep running away from God until he runs (!) out of options. And so on, and so forth. Sometimes one thinks, 'Couldn't he do a lot better?' And then we come to Mary.

Consider Mary's encounter with Gabriel. Gabriel says, 'Greetings, favoured one! The Lord is with you.' The text suggests that Mary is perplexed and bewildered by this greeting, perhaps even suspicious of it: she ponders 'what sort of greeting this might be.' In so far as she is being invited to respond, she is unclear how to do so. Perhaps, Mary senses risk and danger and disruption in God's approach. And, however we interpret what comes next, it is clear her instinct is right: for not only is she told she is favoured by God, but that she is going to have a God-blessed son, the result of being 'overshadowed' by the power of the Holy Spirit.

And yet, as she points out, she is a 'virgin', she is *parthenos*, a maiden, someone who has not known a man. She may be betrothed to Joseph, but (on the basis of the language Luke uses) is quite possibly a girl who hasn't yet had her first period. What response does this child make? 'Here am I, the servant of the Lord; let it be with me according to the word.'

There is simply no doubt that, textually, the images created by this encounter are troubling. A girl meeting God is one thing; a girl being told she will conceive a son via the 'overshadowing' power of the Holy Spirit is another. If this is God's call then it is certainly intrusive, verging on the abusive: power is massively skewed towards God and the whole scene gives the impression of a *fait accompli*. And yet the writer of Luke makes Mary's response significant; Mary's willingness to unite her will and purposes to those of God is no mere afterthought. We encounter how, in Annunciation, *vocare* – call – is close to *vocalis* – voice – in more ways than one. God calls, and Mary finds her voice to respond.

Even if we imagine this angelic message delivered gently, there is no obvious gentleness in it. This call seems lacking in choice; the mood is imperative – 'you will …' This God who chooses Mary comes to her dangerously and edgily. This is not a polite or nice God, but a God of expectations. His expectations go ahead of those he comes to, as if waiting for them to catch up.

I have not sketched perhaps the most attractive pictures of God's calling. This is a God presented as overpowering, terrifying, insistent; a God who chooses individuals and expects obedience. That is, an uncompromising God, who like an intrusive and over-confident parent presumes to know what is best for his children and who values our response perhaps, but expects that response to be 'Yes'. We are, if not in the realm of abuse, close to it.

This is a God I instinctively want to speak against. I want to pile up counter-cases against this God's behaviour – emphasizing the compassion and generosity of God; the gentleness of God.

And yet there is something in this picture of God I've sketched that I want to take seriously. That resonates both in experience, and is actually worthy of serious spiritual consideration.

We rightly want to interrogate this God and many will reject it. Yet there is something authentic in this alien God. This is no domesticated, easy God; this is almost certainly not the kind of god that one would invent for one's own comfort. This God is neither a comfort blanket nor a consumer accessory adopted in order to make one's life feel complete. In an age in which the God who is often preached is one who is friendly, not overly demanding and gentle, this is a God who is alien and strange. And, yet, faithful. This is no Greek god, full of bewildering, yet very human, caprice.

In Scorsese's film version of *The Last Temptation of Christ*, Jesus' opening line is 'God loves me. I know God loves me. I wish he'd stop.' There is something of this in the kind of God who meets Mary. This is the God who calls but who pushes us out so very far from our ordinary human desires and expectations. This is the God who drives Jesus out into the wilderness, who expects Jesus' followers to take up the cross and follow him and who leads Jesus on that bleak road to Jerusalem. This is the God who fills Mary's heart full of rejoicing and yet gifts her a son who pierces her heart. This is the God who is with Moses and yet holds within his grace the shadow of mass slaughter, who pushes his chosen people out into the wilderness for countless years. And somewhere in all this bleakness, in this wilderness and so much night, is the mystery of Love. In this is the startling rigour of our Advent calling: God invites us beyond mere sentiment, beyond comforting feelings and the easy path. He calls us to look – clear-eyed, determinedly – for the coming of the Kingdom. He calls us to prepare, to fast in preparation for the feast.

We are all called, and calling really matters. It matters because it indicates a way of living that resists certain modern pictures of who we should be. These pictures are inclined to view us as individualized economic units whose main work is to maintain a reasonable level of existence for ourselves and ensure that we are not too great a burden on a society comprised of individuals who come together merely for mutual benefit.

On this picture, what matters most is not who we are, what gifts we have, and to what we are drawn, but having a job. A society ordered on this kind of principle will be more concerned about how its citizens can be useful than in helping them discern what they are really about. The purpose of education will entail encouraging young people to pursue paths that are effective, successful and productive rather than seeking to help them figure out who they are, be attentive to what they are drawn to, and discern what they are capable of.

For calling is about being drawn out of oneself towards something: a life, a way of going on. And so, it is also about *response*. It requires commitment, a joining of one's will to that to which one is being drawn. It is about a 'yes' and then giving of ourselves to that direction. And it is never passive.

Travelling with God – the way of vocation – is never, then, merely about a job or even a course of action. It is about the shape and direction of a life and accepting the prospect that this may change us – for either good or ill. We might even get bloody, but within it may lurk true blessing. And if we are not merely working at jobs – even if sometimes in order to protect ourselves and survive we must think that way – we are following a way of life. It is not lifestyle – that great modern idea of what our jobs may allow us to lead – but living. And if God is the true ground of our being and very heart of what we most truly are, her call will always be the primary one; when she comes calling, we may resist, be suspicious and so on, but we can be assured we are being drawn out into our deepest, truest selves.

2

Attending to the Words of the Other: Preaching that Honours the Jewish Texts

RICHARD SUDWORTH

Lost words

In 2007, the *Oxford Junior Dictionary* included a number of new words, largely spawned by the digital revolution, such as 'broadband' and 'chatroom' at the expense of words from the natural world. So 'kingfisher' and 'conker' were among words that disappeared from a major children's English dictionary. In response, the Cambridge English Literature academic Robert Macfarlane published, with illustrator Jackie Morris, *The Lost Words*,[35] a book of acrostic spell-poems. The book is part of a larger project to retain the enchantment of the natural world for a generation in danger of being uncoupled from the wellbeing offered by the beauty and mystery of creation. As the philosopher A. J. Ayer asserted, 'Unless we have a word for something, we are unable to conceive of it.'[36] Our imaginations and ideas are limited by the extent that we have a vocabulary, the bare words, to launch them.

In fundamental ways, the art of preaching involves giving words to a Christian imagination: a narrative of being God's people, the

35 Robert Macfarlane and Jackie Morris, *The Lost Words* (London: Hamish Hamilton, 2017).

36 Quoted in Katharine Norbury, Monday 2 October 2017, *The Guardian*, www.theguardian.com/books/2017/oct/02/the-lost-words-robert-macfarlane-jackie-morris-review [Accessed 9 August 2018].

Church, here and now, in this place. It is necessarily a creative and imaginative process because being God's people, bearing God's calling, goes beyond the here and now and the particularity of this place. And, in turn, the anchor that helps shape and form this Christian imagination are the words we receive in our Scriptures. Without the words of the Bible, we cannot conceive of what it means to be in covenant relationship with the creator God. The spoken words of preaching animate our Scriptures to give colour and form to a renewed Christian imagination much as the spell-poems and illustrations of *The Lost Words* reinvigorate the historic legacy of the vocabulary of the natural world. But both those 'lost words', and the words of the Bible, are not ends in themselves. For Macfarlane and Morris, the reclamation of words like 'adder' and 'magpie' are playfully conjured in poems and acrostics so that children may be drawn back into the wilds of nature. So, preaching that artfully re-presents the legacy of the Bible draws us into the presence of God.

Directing the gaze

In Katharine Norbury's *Guardian* review she recounts asking a magician what he defined as the defining characteristic of his art. 'Directing the gaze', he said. As *The Lost Words* is about enchanting the reader into the wilds of nature, so preaching is about directing the gaze of the congregation to God-in-Christ.

In a sermon broadcast on Radio 4, Damian Howard, the Jesuit Provincial for the Jesuits in Britain, says this about preaching:

> Good preaching draws on what God is already doing in my life. It's not something we can find in theology textbooks, though they will help us understand. The preacher vibrates with the living word of God when [he] knows that God has done great things for [him].[37]

37 Damian Howard SJ, 'A Harvest of Souls', *Sunday Worship*, Sunday 5 October 2014, www.bbc.co.uk/programmes/b04k7b6v [Accessed 9 August 2018].

We can only direct the gaze of the congregation to God-in-Christ if we ourselves are under that gaze, and have done the work with the words of Scripture before God. It is not that the preacher is better, more holy, even if physically we may be six feet above contradiction in a pulpit. Rather, that we have ourselves taken that child-like posture of receiving the gift of God's grace so that the words we speak are a reflection of business done elsewhere, in prayer, study and confession. It is perhaps why the stock sermon phrase 'and I'm preaching this to myself, too', for all that it can be a cheap cliché, at least recognizes the preceding significance of the preacher's own encounter with God-in-Christ.

Growing up in an evangelical home, preaching as 'directing the gaze' to Jesus resonates with all that I have imbibed of my own tradition's sense of the significance of the preaching task. I think of those evangelical parish churches that I have known, and the nonconformist, rural chapel of my in-laws, that challenge the preacher with a sign at eye-level to the pulpit with the injunction of the Greeks that came to Philip in John 12.21, 'we would see Jesus'. A gaze directed to Jesus would confirm the reality of God's preceding gaze over us, and thus draw us into the salvation story that is writ large in the Bible and to which we are invited.

Where my Anglican colleagues of a different tradition may sometimes chafe under the constraints of the lectionary, evangelicals, it is supposed, enjoy the freedom of setting up sermon series around themes and topics. Specific books can be mined for programmatic study, all with the aim of providing a more reflexive engagement that connects that salvation story with the particular needs of a local congregation. The flip-side of this freedom is that we choose those texts we are most comfortable with, and shun the abrasiveness of, say, the prophetic books, the sheer obscurity of Leviticus, or the difficulty of the apocalyptic. The unforeseen consequence is, I observe, a chronic neglect of the Old Testament. Even where the lectionary is most observed, when the Eucharist is now the normative gathering for Sunday worship in the Church of England, how often do our preachers address the Old Testament reading? Indeed, even the lectionary skirts some of the rough edges of Old Testament land-grabs or falters at those thorny moments in the Psalms containing the most blood-curdling vengeance.

It seems to me that we have our very own 'lost words': texts that are no longer known, let alone used within the discourse of the Church. There are stories, and therefore imaginings, of what it means to be covenant people of God, and intrinsically human and failing people, that are in danger of being unavailable to us. Right at the heart of this concern there is an ethical charge of how Christians are to articulate the *Jewishness* of so much of our Scriptures and the tradition that provides inextricable roots to the Church.

For all of my ordained ministry, I have been in parishes that have been dominated by other faith communities: Muslim, especially, but also Sikh and Hindu groups. Church life has been in contexts where people 'do God'. Living and ministering in such contexts brings a sharp apologetic schooling, whether conscious or subconscious. Local Christians find ways of articulating both similarity and difference, however well informed that may be. A popular distinction from Muslim beliefs among Christians is the shorthand that 'Christianity is a religion of grace; Islam is a religion of law'. It is a distinction that has a grain of truth but that belies a whole world of complexity. That simple dichotomy ignores both the rich Christian tradition of law as well as some of the intimations of grace in Muslim traditions such as Sufism. Is 'law' becoming another lost word for Anglican Christians, forgetful of Thomas Aquinas, Calvin, and our very own Richard Hooker? This question's ethical dimension in relation to Muslims is actually a question about our very own identity. If Christianity is a religion of grace and not of law, then what on earth do we do with the Old Testament and 'the law'? What has Jerusalem to do with Rome? The slide towards an implicit contemporary version of the heresy of Marcionism, the rejection of the Old Testament, is very real.

A sacrament of otherness

This is the paradox that I have found myself in, working and ministering among Muslims in Birmingham: encountering faith others has meant I have had to dig deeper into my own scriptural and Christian traditions and become much more attentive to the Jewishness of our roots, and the responsibility of faithfully preaching that inheritance. Cardinal Walter Kaspar has described Judaism as a 'sacrament of otherness' to the Church.[38] If a sacrament is a visible sign of the invisible reality of God's grace, then, according to Kaspar, the encounter with Judaism offers the prospect of the reception of God's grace to the Church. Wrestling with 'the law', the Old Testament, and the ongoing 'sign' of Jewish presence throughout the whole Bible, is a means of receiving the gift of God. The Jewishness of our texts is simultaneously a strangeness to gentile Christians who are not held by the particularities of the old covenant, and an intimate affinity. In embracing these texts, in their otherness, we join a cosmic story of God's redemptive purposes, and come to know the mystery of the wholly Other that is YAHWEH. This sacramental move is specific to the Hebrew texts, and the faith of the Jewish people from whom the Christian faith is indebted, but offers a paradigm for how 'the other', more generally, can become the vehicle for God's instruction to us.

In the salvation story of our Scriptures, we are faced with the double move of a God who works from the particular to the universal: through the covenant people of Israel, and outwards

38 Walter Cardinal Kasper, 'Address on the 37th Anniversary of *Nostra Aetate*', 28 October 2002, www.ccjr.us/dialogika-resources/documents-and-statements/roman-catholic/kasper/650-wk02oct28 (accessed 9 August 2018). I am grateful to Bishop Michael Ipgrave for pointing out this reference and for his own work on developing the idea of the 'sacrament of otherness' for Anglican Christian–Jewish relations.

to the world through the Church. The universal trajectory of the mission of God means that the Church can never circumscribe the limits of divine action, while God chooses to work in the concreteness of covenant and through a people that repeatedly fail. The particularities of both the glory and the hubris of the Old Testament nation of Israel should feel familiar and close to home. It is at once our story, but strange, other, with the Christological reading we bring. Part of the prior work that Howard alludes to in the task of preaching involves settling into a certain security that our texts, like our God, are both irresistibly strange and mysteriously close. The Bible, and the preached word, are comforting as well as disruptive. As Walter Brueggemann exclaims, looking back to Barth's great theological project, 'The God of the Bible is not "somewhere else," but is given only in, with, and under the text itself.'[39] It is just this sort of commitment by Brueggemann that charges his studies of the Old Testament texts with a sense of the 'restless character of the text that refuses excessive closure', 'reflective of the One who is its main Character, who also refuses tameness or systematization.'[40]

It is at this point that I would draw attention to those pregnant moments of sermon preparation. Even if our prayerful reflections are luxuriating in unhurried time, without the demands of dinner preparation or the significant attentions of family, I know my own mind is often clamouring with distraction. I would confess to the easy temptation of the domestication of the text; the shortcut to the preaching nugget that asserts control. This is the point at which the more considered rhetoric slips into shop-worn preaching as marketing. The Bible is difficult, necessarily so, and the Old Testament strange, but sheering off its sharp corners, or evading them entirely, is a dereliction of the preacher's vocation. This vocation is decidedly *spiritual*, in being an opportunity to be before God-in-Christ, and *ethical*,

39 Walter Brueggemann, *Theology of the Old Testament: Testimony, Disputes, Advocacy* (Minneapolis, MN: Fortress Press, 1997), p. 19.

40 Brueggemann, *Theology of the Old Testament*, p. 42.

in orienting us to the primary other that we encounter in the Jewishness of Scripture.

Those insecurities during sermon preparation that I experience can lead to me articulating sermons that are the equivalent of fast food: easily reproduced but inherently unhealthy and insubstantial. This is not an argument for obscurantism or elitism in our preaching but, to perhaps continue the analogy, it is a claim for attention to origins, source and integrity. A neglect of the difficulty of the Bible produces a caricature such as 'the God of the Old Testament', and inexorably leads to a picture of the Jews as legalistic and obstinate. It is a beguiling temptation because a shoring up of that primary other as deserving of our scorn enables the Church to be bolstered in self-satisfaction. And who among us preachers wishes to leave our congregations less than satisfied or affirmed after our sermons? When our expositions denigrate the old covenant and the Jewish people, we fall into an age-old sin that has come to be termed 'preaching with contempt'.[41] Whether it is John of Chrysostom in the fourth century or Martin Luther in the sixteenth century, there is a long trail of preaching in the Church that sets Jewishness as a negative foil to Christianity.

The Jewishness of our Bible texts is, clearly, not confined to the Old Testament, and is apparent in often abrasive and contradictory form within the New Testament. The tension of affinity and difference, strangeness and intimacy is replayed in the new Church's negotiations with its Jewish inheritance:

> This process, begun by Paul, of presenting Jewish messianic ideas to a gentile audience – assigning universal significance to the traditions of one particular community – was not straightforward.
>
> All sorts of tensions were set up, the results of which are still with us.[42]

41 Jules Isaac, *The Teaching of Contempt: Christian Roots of Anti-Semitism* (New York: Holt, Rinehart & Winston, 1964).

42 Ann Conway-Jones, 'The New Testament: Jewish or Gentile?',unpublished paper given at the British Association of Jewish Studies conference, July 2018.

As we read the New Testament, we are bystanders to a messy and unresolved conversation about the Jewishness of the Way of Christ, with its own insecurities and polemics. Eliding such complexities may well simplify Scripture, but at best it risks overlooking the Jewish challenge and gift to the Church; and at worst, demonizing the Jew. Thus, a myriad of sermon archetypes are spawned: the Pharisees as ciphers for Jewish legalism and dishonest plotting, the Jews as Christ-murderers, or the Jews as ethnically enclosed nationalists. Naturally, these and other stereotypes are all offered in contradistinction to the Church that is full of grace and freedom, untrammelled by regulation and petty legalism, or the Church as innocent victim of imperial power, and disclosed to the whole world, especially those on the margins of society.[43] These are tempting tropes for the preacher, and too often heard from our pulpits, but they are a travesty of history as well as of faithful exposition. Much like old-style Hollywood cowboy films, where the 'bad guys' are immediately discernible by their black Stetson hats, Christian preaching has signalled its own simplistic binaries. Such binaries dehumanize self and other even as they seek to orient and secure.

The Easter God and His Easter People

Bishop John V. Taylor, with Max Warren and Bishop Kenneth Cragg, was part of the 'Christian Presence' school of Anglican missionary-scholars that brought attention to the world Church and the religious-other into the mainstream of the Church of England in the latter half of the twentieth century. Taylor, also an accomplished poet, became famous for his preaching while Bishop of Winchester, and a number of notable collections of those sermons were published during his lifetime. The posthumously

43 See Amy-Jill Levine, 'Bearing False Witness: Common Errors Made About Early Judaism', in *The Jewish Annotated New Testament* (Oxford: Oxford University Press, 2011), pp. 501–4. This edition is an excellent resource offering scholarly Jewish perspectives on the New Testament and its context to Christians.

published collection *The Easter God and His Easter People* contains a sermon that is emblematic of the way that Taylor was attuned to the tension of hearing the strangeness, the challenge of the other, in the biblical text.

'The True Kingdom' offers reflections on Jesus' encounter with the Syrophoenician woman in Matthew 15.[44] Recalling that these sermons were delivered in a cathedral setting, Taylor begins with a provocative flourish: 'People who have a strong religious faith are naturally very disturbed when God appears to change his mind.'[45] Grabbing our attention from the start he then steers his listener towards an orthodox understanding of revelation as a 'discontinuity': where God says or does something new. For Taylor, the charged exchange between Jesus and the Syrophoenician woman is just such a moment and, most wonderfully, this foreign woman has been the agent of that discontinuity. Jesus himself changes his mind, comes to a new position on the scope of the good news, because of this pushy pagan: 'O woman, daughter of Tyre, with your cheeky courage, great is your faith, for it launched the universal, world-wide, Catholic Church.'[46]

Part of Taylor's skill lies in the way he alternates between the provocative and the scandalous, and the steady setting of context within church orthodoxy. He is not ashamed to 'teach': to provide background to the text and context, and root this in orthodox doctrine. But all this is done with a light touch, and a poet's eye for images and parallels. So, the hitherto landlocked ministry of Jesus is contrasted with their location in the port environs of Tyre and Sidon, with Jesus gazing out to the broad expanse of the sea, and the vast empire of Rome: 'The short visit to the seaside was over. But the sea had flowed into the minds of the disciples.'[47] He is attentive to the salvation history

44 John V. Taylor, 'The True Kingdom', in *The Easter God and His Easter People* (London: Continuum, 2003), pp. 95–9.

45 Taylor, 'The True Kingdom', p. 95.

46 Taylor, 'The True Kingdom', p. 97.

47 Taylor, 'The True Kingdom', p. 97.

overarching this encounter, from a very Jewish story that begins to branch out, anticipating the missionary voyages of the first apostles.

Then Taylor takes us to another port scene, and another reversal. This time we learn about Peter and Cornelius in Acts 10, and the consolidation of the mission to the gentiles that requires Peter to have his mind changed by a Roman centurion. Peter is not portrayed as a religious pedant, concerned only for the rules, but as a man who has a high regard for the truth – 'he could not play fast and loose with one of the definitive ordinances of their faith.' And notice that poetic thread recurring: 'But Peter had felt the sea sweeping in past the old bastions.'[48] Taylor gently walks us through this decisive moment for the Church, bringing us in touch with the feelings and dilemmas facing the participants to that first event, and directing our gaze to the expansive love of God. It is important that Taylor does not resort to an anodyne message about God's good news being inclusive: the hospitality of God, here, faces up to the particularity and significance of the covenant promises to the Jews. There is genuine jeopardy; truth and revelation matter and should cohere, but God in his radical freedom will out!

I believe that Taylor models for us in this sermon, which appropriately reflects his theological oeuvre, an ecclesial-consciousness that is alive to the gift and challenge of the other. A serious attention to the Jewishness of our Scriptures helps us receive the otherness that is elsewhere apparent in Scripture and in our world. If Jesus could change his mind because of the wilful disputation of a foreign, religious-other, how might we as fallible Christians need to hear the voice of the other? This does not give licence for 'new revelations' Taylor's careful exegesis has not built up the prospect of a sanctified relativism, but he has prodded the Church into some interdependence and humility. At an important juncture in the sermon, Taylor addresses the Syrophoenician woman: 'Let us never forget

48 Taylor, 'The True Kingdom', p. 98.

that you and I and virtually the whole of Christendom are the dogs.'[49] Before we are tempted to regard the Jewish covenant as ethnically exclusive, and wrong-footing any tendency to moral superiority, he agrees with Jesus' rather politically incorrect language that puts most of the Church, and himself first and foremost, under that judgement. This, arguably, is the vital lesson for preaching that endeavours to wrestle with the strange other in Scripture: locate oneself in the place of the stranger, the outsider, the undeserving.

Avoiding 'kitsch'

In Milan Kundera's celebrated novel *The Unbearable Lightness of Being*, written in communist Czechoslovakia, he goes on one of his typical philosophical excursions reflecting on the nature of *kitsch*. For Kundera, totalitarian regimes exemplify the meaning of kitsch in their public events gesturing at unity, no more so than during the May Day parades. No questions are possible and 'the dictatorship of the heart reigns supreme'.[50] A politician kissing a baby in front of the cameras is a moment of kitsch because critical judgement is suspended and one is moved not by the kissing of a child but by the *ideal* of the kissing of a child. All doubt, irony and particularity are erased in the realm of kitsch; everything is tidy, and there are no loose ends.

Sam Wells has suggested that the counter-weight to sentimentality in stories and illustrations is to be 'tightly moored to the cerebral argument or firmly rooted in visceral, primal, human reality'.[51] I would argue that not just our stories and illustrations, but our choice and use of Scripture, can veer into the sentimental, the kitsch, even the totalitarian, when

49 Taylor, 'The True Kingdom', p. 97.

50 Milan Kundera, *The Unbearable Lightness of Being* (London: Faber & Faber, 1984), p. 250.

51 Samuel Wells, *Learning to Dream Again: Rediscovering the Heart of God* (Norwich: Canterbury Press, 2013), p. xiii.

unmoored from the breadth of the Bible and where serious attention is not given to its difficulty. It is part of the gift of the Old Testament that its visceral, untidy, very human face is offered to us. The heroes and heroines of the Old Testament are a motley bunch, as are those first apostles, and so are we. We don't need to find a smoothed-out path that neatly explains away the conquest of Jericho, or that can satisfactorily account for the change of mind of Jesus in Matthew 15. But we ignore those questions at our peril, as if we were responsible for doing some tidying up work to Scriptures that would be much better excised from the canon.

In my world of interreligious encounter, I am accustomed to have in mind a helpful truism: 'if my Muslim/Sikh/Hindu/Jewish neighbour were in the room now, what would they think of what I say?' It is a good prompt, and one that should not necessarily curtail every unpleasing statement. Sometimes we have to say tough things to our friends and neighbours. I wonder, though, especially in our encounter with the Jewishness of our Scripture, how many of us as we preach would be minded to imagine a Jew sitting and listening to our sermons? This primary 'other', indeed a sacrament of otherness, highlighting the strangeness and familiarity of YAHWEH, and pointing to the fragile openness of the Church, needs to be heard. Our task is an exegetical one, involving the intellectual craft of mining our salvation story in the Bible, and also an ethical one, not just for the good of the other, but for the integrity and good of the Church. May we recover lost words in all our parish churches.

A Sermon for Christmas: A Song Sang Out, Across the Starlit Way

FRANCES WARD

A dark, bleak time. A wilderness the way;
cold and unrelenting was the night.
Come with tender mercy, Christ, we pray.

It seemed all heaven and earth had passed away.
No love. No warmth. No rest. No friendly sight.
A dark, bleak time. A wilderness the way.

For you with child, awaiting the dawn of day
The gentle knowing moon gave holy light.
Come with tender mercy, Christ, we pray.

A single flame with steady, circling ray
Brought comfort on that terrifying night.
A dark, bleak time. A wilderness the way.

A song sang out, across the starlit way.
The angels' shout announced the daystar bright.
Come with tender mercy, Christ, we pray.

And you, Christchild, guide our feet this day;
To those who dwell in darkness, give your light.
Through dark, bleak times – through wilderness – the way,
Come with tender mercy, Christ, we pray.

© Frances Ward (unpublished)

Imagine you're far from home – a home you've left behind because you must. You're travelling and it's hard. All you see during the day are strange faces in strange towns, who view you with suspicion. There's no one to trust, no one who cares. The world feels a dark, bleak place. You're fearful and anxious. The child inside you will be born soon, and you have no idea where.

Such was the experience of Mary as she travelled with Joseph to be registered. A familiar story of long ago – but relevant today. Mary stands for so many now, and through the ages. People on the move, far from the security they crave.

A dark, bleak time. A wilderness the way;
cold and unrelenting was the night.
Come with tender mercy, Christ, we pray.

Except, of course, there was no Christ, as yet, to pray to. Mary had little idea of what her child would mean to the world. As the story goes, she had heard from an angel that she was favoured of God. She had some inkling that the child would be different, special – but how could she know his significance?

Thoughts far from her mind, as now, weary to her core, she longed for warmth, for rest. She was at the limit of her endurance.

It seemed all heaven and earth had passed away.
No love. No warmth. No rest. No friendly sight.
A dark, bleak time. A wilderness the way.

Another step, and then another. Along that dark, interminable road. The steady human stream of the highway had died down, now that night had come. 'But more dangerous', thought Joseph. Her pregnancy made them vulnerable. 'Or more safe, perhaps,' he thought. For they looked poor, a couple with nothing to give. Not worth the effort.

The road was rough, but as the moon grew bright, the ruts

threw shadows. She stumbled less. She took a moment to glance up. The familiar round face had silver rings around. She gained courage.

For you with child, awaiting the dawn of day
The gentle knowing moon gave holy light.
Come with tender mercy, Christ, we pray.

The lights of a town! She sighed, and paused again. May this be the place. Please, dear God. As they drew near, it was busy. 'Too busy', muttered Joseph. There was nightlife; people milling around on the streets; the odd market stall still trading – food, trinkets for the travellers.

They tried one place. No luck. Another. And another. And then someone took pity on her. 'There's a stable out the back. Rough. The animals'll keep you warm.' He gave them a candle, and Joseph pulled the blanket out across the straw.

A single flame with steady, circling ray
Brought comfort on that terrifying night.
A dark, bleak time. A wilderness the way.

It wasn't a long labour. All that walking had helped. Shaken him down, firmly into her pelvis. Joseph – good, kind, solid Joseph – calmly asked the wife to help, and stayed through it all.

The pain came and went in waves. Her young body did what it had to do.

And there he was. Exquisite. Healthy. Content.

As she fed him, the world stood still. The animals stopped their chewing. The dog stood to attention by the door. It seemed as though all creation had gathered itself in one momentous silent holding of breath – and then, like the great outrush of tension, the world came alive. With raucous, vibrant, joyous life.

Mary knew she had given birth to hope. Hope that this tired, dark world yearned to receive. Hope born with this new life. Hope born of the knowledge of the love of God.

A song sang out, across the starlit way.
The angels' shout announced the daystar bright.
Come with tender mercy, Christ, we pray.

As dawn glowed gold across the Eastern sky, the door pushed open to show three hesitant, eager faces. Shepherds who had hurried from the hills. They told of a great light across the sky; of angels singing a song that stopped their hearts with joy. They knew something extraordinary had happened. A new bright light had dawned. A light and life such as the world had never seen.

And you, Christchild, guide our feet this day;
To those who dwell in darkness, give your light.
Through dark, bleak times – through wilderness – the way,
Come with tender mercy, Christ, we pray.

And we, this holy night, who have gathered to this crib, are bathed in that same light. We receive the gift of hope, born of the love of God. This is a gift we are asked to share, for many dwell in darkness today. In fear. Caught in despair and helplessness. Heavy laden with fatigue.

God's gift of hope is ours, ours to give and share. Received this night as blessing, it's ours to take out into the future, to bring to the dark places of the world, for the Christchild is born to us this night.

And you, Christchild, guide our feet this day;
To those who dwell in darkness, give your light.
Through dark, bleak times – through wilderness – the way,
Come with tender mercy, Christ, we pray.

3

Attending to the Holy Spirit: Preaching 'Each in Our Own Language'

JOEL LOVE

Fresh out of theological college, a curate's first sermons can often be lengthy, dense, and filled with theological detail or quotations from the Greek. But such sermons do not always connect with the congregation, even if the deacon in question can definitely connect when telling the story of her faith journey, or when leading a Bible study group. Finding the right register or style for a sermon can be difficult. Ideally the preacher will want to choose a style that fits both the content of her sermon and the congregation that she is preaching to. This is particularly important when the festival or day evokes some complex emotions. And when there are cultural or linguistic differences between the preacher and members of the congregation.

Having reflected together about these specific difficulties, I was impressed when our curate got up to preach on Mothering Sunday and began her sermon by singing a traditional Yoruba song that her mother had sung to her when she was a child. The simple melody she sang came as a surprise when we were expecting the spoken word. There was an intimacy and a vulnerability about it that were disarming. And it had a freedom or unplanned quality that made it all the more immediate. The congregation was rapt, and she held our attention for the rest of her sermon.

Our curate's sermon connected with the congregation because

it acknowledged the complex mix of personal memories and associations that are present in church on Mothering Sunday, and it successfully interpreted from several traditions (Scripture, personal upbringing) in a relatable way. Preaching that attends to the Holy Spirit will be fully present in the moment. It will be firmly located in the tradition or traditions that inform it. And, most of all, it will be characterized by the qualities that are associated with the Holy Spirit: spontaneity and freedom, passion for truth, convicting of sin and righteousness, pointing to Christ, bearing fruit, and building others up. In this chapter, I will suggest that our preaching will be most effective when we are in the moment, in the tradition, and most importantly when we are in the Spirit. Time is the medium in which the Holy Spirit writes, and Scripture is one record of this revelation. But life is another, and the good preacher will need to 'read' both life and Scripture if she is to make sense of what the Spirit is saying.

Peter's sermon on the day of Pentecost offers an excellent model for preaching that is attentive to the Spirit. Here we have a sermon about the Holy Spirit that is explicitly empowered by the Spirit. It is 'in the moment' because it acknowledges the reaction of the crowd to the Pentecost event, and because it expresses in real time Peter's own perplexity. It also bears witness to the resurrection as a simultaneously recent and world-changing event. Peter preaches 'in the tradition' when he quotes the prophecy of Joel and the psalms of David. For Peter's listeners on the day of Pentecost, this was a shared tradition, but elsewhere in the Acts of the Apostles we find other approaches where such a common tradition is absent. And Peter's sermon is very emphatically 'in the Spirit' as he attends to what the Spirit is revealing both in time and in the Scriptures. It is the Spirit who helps him to improvise, and this is true even though the account of his sermon was written down later. (For the purposes of this chapter, I am assuming that something like this sermon was preached by someone called Peter or one of the other disciples when the Holy Spirit was first poured out upon them.)

Peter opens his Pentecost sermon by acknowledging what his listeners are thinking, including the weirdness of the situation. His words can even be seen as a joke at his own expense: 'Indeed, these are not drunk, as you suppose, for it is only nine o'clock in the morning' (Acts 2.15). From here, he proceeds on the basis of the shared cultural points of reference that he and his listeners share, which in this case are the Jewish Scriptures (the tradition) and the recent events of that Passover in Jerusalem (the present moment). The fact that these events are still topical is shown by Peter's reference to them as things that 'you yourselves know'. Peter begins with the perplexity of his hearers and shows that this is precisely where God is being revealed. This move is effective because Peter feels the same perplexity in the moment. It is not just a rhetorical ploy. The promised Spirit has come, and we can detect the wonder in Peter's voice, as he works out (as it were) in real time what has occurred. Subsequent sermons in the Acts of the Apostles have a similar quality, such Stephen's exclamation: 'Look ... I see the heavens opened and the Son of Man standing at the right hand of God!' (Acts 7.56). This works best when the excitement is spontaneous and unfeigned. So the preacher needs to have 'a heart that's exploring the mysteries of God and God's reign into which we want to draw others'; a life of prayer that practises the presence of God in the present moment.[52]

The surprising nature of the Pentecost event leaves the bystanders 'amazed and perplexed, saying to one another, "What does this mean?"' (Acts 2.12). Very often, our preaching fails to either pose or respond to this simple question. And yet this must be the question on our hearers' minds when they come to church on a Sunday (or listen to the news on a Monday, or read the paper on a Saturday). What happens inside our

52 John-Francis Friendship, *Enfolded in Christ: The Inner Life of a Priest* (Norwich: Canterbury Press, 2018), p. xxii.

churches should be permeable to the world outside, just as the world is permeable to the Holy Spirit. Our preaching should therefore take local, national and international events into account. This kind of sermon was demonstrated dramatically in the BBC television series *Broken*, when Sean Bean's character preaches about the evils of gambling machines and unleashes a local campaign against them. Occasions for wonder and thanksgiving should be held up in our preaching, alongside prophetic challenges and words of comfort or healing. On every occasion, we should be asking 'What does this mean?' The Bible gives us licence to refer to the breadth of human behaviour, the natural world, our culture and history, as well as the large-scale geopolitical events that we read about in the news. People arrive in church with a range of experiences and intimations of the divine already. We should expect the Holy Spirit to have been at work in their lives, and we can appeal to these intimations. But here the preacher should tread with care, for it is holy ground. And what of those people who bring hurt or anger into church with them? Our preaching should always be sensitive to such needs among our hearers. But the only way to guarantee this is for the preacher to know her people and their sufferings well, by being with them and in the Spirit, in the moment.

Part of the problem for us when taking the sermons of the New Testament (and this basically means the sermons of the Acts of the Apostles) as our model is that we confuse two elements that happen to overlap there, but that for us are distinct. The death and resurrection of Jesus are definitive moments in our salvation history ('in the tradition'), and must be rehearsed again, and again, as the story of the exodus is rehearsed again and again throughout Scripture. But, for Peter, the resurrection was also a recent event and therefore topical ('in the moment'). In the New Testament, 'Scripture' refers only to the law and the prophets, while the events described in the Gospels and the Acts of the Apostles have the character of recent or current affairs. This is no longer the case for us, so we must find other – more proximate – instances of God at work, and point to these in our preaching along with the resurrection. This is what it means for our preaching to be in time. The sermons of the Old Testament prophets look forward to the fulfilment of God's promises, and the sermons of the New Testament bear witness to the resurrection. The sermons of Jesus have a different character because he is the eternal Word, whereas we rely on the Holy Spirit enabling us to point to the Word. In a Trinitarian economy, the Word is never heard without the Spirit. God's Spirit is in the world alongside us as she was for the first apostles: in life as well as in Scripture. Testimonies to God's work in our own lives and in the lives of our communities possess the same kind of immediacy. This is why an intimation of God's loving care in a Yoruba lullaby can speak to a congregation of diverse churchgoers on a Mothering Sunday in Kent. These (admittedly lesser) instances of the power of God at work in our time and place will be the springboard that allows us to retell the story of God's love and faithfulness, while pointing to the cross and empty tomb of Scripture. We must not look for the living among the dead, but for signs of resurrection in the here and now.

Peter's sermon shows that God's revelation is not happening somewhere else, but here and now. Just as the curate found that the sharing of a personal experience provided a good opening for a sermon on Mothering Sunday, so also Peter speaks from his immediate experience. He takes what is happening in the present – no matter how unfamiliar or surprising – and shows how it fits with what he and his hearers already know of God from within their tradition. Peter is making sense of what has happened not only for his hearers, but for himself as well. He reaches instinctively for what he already knows of God from the tradition, and he weaves it together in this way: first, we know that God can pour out his Spirit on anyone, as the prophet Joel had foretold; second, that God uses 'signs' to 'attest' to his chosen one; and third, that the greatest of these signs is the resurrection, to which Peter and the other disciples are witnesses. Peter concludes: 'Therefore let the entire house of Israel know with certainty that God has made him both Lord and Messiah, this Jesus whom you crucified' (Acts 2.36).

For us, these last words ring with the echoes of centuries of anti-Semitism. But this is to hear Peter's words anachronistically. By using 'house of Israel' and 'Messiah', Peter is claiming that his message is consistent with the Judaism of his day. He is saying that the good news is not only comprehensible within the worldview of his hearers (within the tradition), but that it actually speaks to their dearest hopes for the future. He does not flatter his hearers, or leave them with a warm fuzzy feeling, however. There is something scandalous about associating the Hebrew 'Messiah' with the Greek 'Lord' (at least in Luke's telling of the story). And to say that a crucified man was God's chosen Messiah was only to compound the perplexity of the crowd. It is as if Peter wants to say that the bewildering happenings of Pentecost are a sign of something even more astonishing, and that the congruence of these events points to something amazing and mysterious in the very nature of God.

There are two almost contradictory things happening in Peter's use of language in Acts 2, which are repeated in other instances of preaching from within the biblical record. On the one hand, it is simple and straightforward, easily accessible to his hearers, 'devout Jews from every nation under heaven' who hear him speaking 'in the native language of each' (Acts 2.5–6). Yet at the same time, what Peter says is incredibly challenging to his hearers' view of themselves and of God. When Paul proclaims God as creator and judge before an audience of Athenians later in the Acts of the Apostles, he does so in the words of their own poet, a representative of their unique tradition (Acts 17.28). And Paul preaches to the Athenians without naming Jesus directly: 'a man whom he has appointed, and of this he has given assurance to all by raising him from the dead' (Acts 17.31). But in spite of these sensitivities to language and tradition, Paul's message is equally disorienting for his hearers: 'When they heard of the resurrection of the dead, some scoffed; but others said "We will hear you again about this"' (Acts 17.32). Jesus similarly refuses to give his hearers exactly what they want. The saying 'Let anyone with ears listen!' (echoing Isaiah 6.8–10) alludes to the mystery of God's Kingdom that cannot be pinned down and which exceeds the simple stories that Jesus tells in everyday language. We are supposed to be perplexed in the face of the mystery of God, who is always calling us to a deeper personal engagement. Like the disciples, the Pharisees and the crowds, the hearers of a perplexing sermon will feel by turns mystified, targeted, and hungry for more. It has the quality of turning the present moment and their tradition upside-down.

Tentatively piecing together Scripture and life is the model established by Peter in Acts 2. This was the role that Jesus predicted for the Spirit when he said: 'do not worry about how you are to defend yourselves or what you are to say; for the Holy Spirit will teach you at that very hour what you ought to say' (Luke 12.11–12). And again in John 16.12–14:

> I still have many things to say to you, but you cannot bear them now. When the Spirit of truth comes, he will guide you into all the truth; for he will not speak on his own, but will speak whatever he hears, and he will declare to you the things that are to come. He will glorify me, because he will take what is mine and declare it to you.

At its best, preaching is a place where the Holy Spirit combines improvisation with revelation. This is an area fraught with danger and tension, but also excitement. Both preacher and hearers will need that other gift of the Holy Spirit, the discernment of spirits (1 Corinthians 12.10).

We have seen that Peter is fully in the moment and firmly situated in the tradition when he preaches his Pentecost sermon. But more than this, he is 'filled with the Holy Spirit'

(Acts 2.4). The Spirit of God does not draw attention to herself, but to Christ. The Spirit bears witness to the truth. So to hear what the Spirit is saying is to attend all the more closely to the moment and to the tradition, meaning that the preacher needs to be immersed in both. The preacher should have a genuine experience of being drawn deeper into the life of God, and a willingness to speak honestly about this experience. Humour and wonder will emerge from this embodied experience, and with them an openness to the Spirit's guidance, and discernment about what this means in a given context or moment, and in a given tradition. Preaching is thus a facet of discipleship, which must come first. And if the preacher is a disciple, her life itself will speak of Christ.[53] Only in Christ, of course, will this being 'in the Spirit' be totally congruent. All of this amounts to a realization that homiletics (the art of preaching) is a branch of pneumatology (the doctrine of the Holy Spirit). It is the Spirit of God who bears witness to Christ, who takes what is hidden and reveals it to us, and who enables us to communicate the gospel in a variety of voices and contexts. This does not necessarily mean that preaching must be *ex tempore*. Faithful improvisation 'in the Spirit' can take place in the library or in the preacher's study as well as in Lectio Divina, prayer meetings and Bible studies. What matters is that the preacher improvises 'in the Spirit', in the present, and in the tradition.

The characteristics of preaching in the Spirit will be congruent with what we know about the Spirit: varied, challenging, and bearing witness to Christ. Peter's sermon is full of variety: a range of rhetorical techniques and tones, as well as a variety of languages, are present on that day of Pentecost. Beginning with humour and wonder, Peter moves through tentative interpretation towards explanation, followed by accusation and direct appeal. Many of the sermons in the Acts of the Apostles are provocative and end abruptly, crying out for a response. But

53 As one of the religious interviewed in Wim Wenders's recent film *Pope Francis: A Man of His Word* put it, 'his life is a sermon'.

attending to the Spirit may equally lead us to preach sermons from the holy ground of contemplation, or from a place of pain and despair. Qoheleth, the biblical book of 'the Preacher', refrains from offering any easy answers, and the Spirit often leads people into the wilderness, or meets them there. And, of course, there are sermons that sound like ecstatic cries of joy. So why do we not preach like this? And why do we not go to church with the eager expectation of hearing something real and fresh from God in the present moment?

The nature of God is reflected in the sheer variety and creativity of the approaches to be found. Living in time as we do, humans will often experience God's self-revelation as an unfolding story. But God also delights in paradox and mystery, which humans experience as poetry and wonder. God is truth, which humans discover as theory and concept. God is love, which for humans translates into a wide range of emotions (most of which are painful and costly). God is creator, so the variety of ways in which we can speak about God will be endless. And God's self-revelation is always congruent with his being, so preaching that is attentive to the Holy Spirit will be 'fitting' in terms of both the medium and the message.

Because we believe that God is revealed in all of creation, we must expect to hear from God in one another's voices, in all our diversity and idiosyncrasy. This, too, is part of the Spirit's freedom. And the Spirit is associated from the beginning with diversity. Disciples male and female bear witness to their experience of the Spirit of Jesus[54] in the Acts of the Apostles, and this diversity of voices is what allows the gospel to be proclaimed to 'all tribes and peoples and languages' (Revelation 7.9). The embodied experiences of gender, age, ethnicity, social class, and the diversity of human physical and mental ways of being must all enter into the Church's preaching because 'the Spirit [has] no ambition to homogenize the peoples of the world into a uniform Christian culture. On the contrary, he [intends]

54 'This Jesus God raised up, and of that all of us are witnesses' (Acts 2.32), and see Acts 16.6–7.

to bridge cultures and to overcome the alienation they create without eroding the diversity they represent'.[55] Later, the apostle Paul would come to the realization that 'there are varieties of gifts, but the same Spirit; and there are varieties of services, but the same Lord; and there are varieties of activities, but it is the same God who activates all of them in everyone. To each is given the manifestation of the Spirit for the common good' (1 Corinthians 12.4–7).

And, as Jesus also told us, the Spirit convicts people of sin (John 16.8–11). There are no shortcuts to the direct appeal with which Peter ends his sermon. Without engaging the humour, emotions and lived experiences of the hearer, 'evangelistic' sermons that call for an immediate response will meet with only limited success. Along with the poets, lawgivers and storytellers of the Hebrew Scriptures, the prophets use colourful language and performance art to show how corrupt, hypocritical and ridiculous the people's behaviour has become. Sometimes their humour has a biting edge, as in the names that Hosea gives to his children. At other times, the humour is tinged with sadness, even lament. Something like this is happening when St Peter starts with his hearers' laughter and ends by showing that they are complicit in the rejection of God's chosen one (Acts 2.36). A hearer who recognizes herself in the humour of a sermon may be more likely to feel convicted by it, and then ready to repent (see Acts 2.38). But notice that Peter only calls his hearers to repentance after they have asked 'what should we do?' (Acts 2.37). Preaching participates in the world and leads to dialogue and transformation. Outcomes such as these are not in the control of the preacher, but of the Holy Spirit. And just as Peter's sermon in Acts 2 is eschatological (he quotes the prophecy of Joel about the 'day of the Lord'), so also our preaching must anticipate the eschaton. We must remain open, and trust the Holy Spirit to add to our number. As preachers, we must attend

55 Roy Clements, *Turning the World Upside Down: Acts in Action* (Leicester: Inter-Varsity Press, 1998), p. 22.

to the Spirit in and through our lives and the Scriptures. This is the same Spirit who comes with a 'rush of violent' wind and 'divided tongues of fire', always full of surprises but always bearing witness to the Word who is present in every moment.

A Sermon for Epiphany: Strange Gifts from the East

RICHARD SUDWORTH

'What was all that about?' We are entitled to ask that very question each year as we surface from the overindulging amid the rubble of unwrapped presents and moulting Christmas trees. Sometimes our very remembrance of the Christmas story itself has taken on so many layers of sentimentality and seasonal mythology that we could be forgiven for missing the heart of the story. Epiphany follows quickly after and is no less laden with distraction. Were they kings? Were there three of them? Were they called Balthasar, Melchior and Gaspar? Did they arrive on camels in the light of a freakish star and lay their gifts alongside the shepherds and their sheep? And, as my inner ten-year-old still wants to sing, did they travel by taxi, car and scooter?

Well, I hope the reading of the Matthew's Gospel, the only one to mention this visit, at least answers some of those questions. We learn that they are *magi*: scholars practised in the arts of astrology from Persia. What our nativity plays get absolutely right is the utter strangeness of these visitors to the infant Jesus. We have images of them in fine clothes, bejewelled, and all with an ethnic twist. The magi are truly weird actors in this play, coming from offstage and giving us the sights, sounds and smells of some place that is decidedly elsewhere. What we too easily overlook, though, is the utter scandal and provocation of these Eastern visitors. They are not just *strange*, they are *wrong*.

In the Old Testament, Hebrew Bible, the magi are those interpreters of dreams in the Babylonian kingdom that Daniel reveals as false and powerless in the face of the one, true God, YAHWEH. Early Jewish, Christian, and even Greek writings all point to a very negative perception of magi. There are frequent injunctions in the Old Testament forbidding the seeking of guidance through the stars, just in case the mention of magi was not enough for us to be alerted to the arrival of guests that are unexpected in more ways than one. Indeed, if you were to write an account of Jesus as Messiah, the anointed of God, approving mention of stargazing magi would be the least helpful elements to include in your story.

What we have here in this opening section of Matthew is something of the in-breaking of God's revelation to all peoples. The magi, in essence, are the dodgy outsiders who still get in on the act. The reading from Isaiah 60 offers hints and foreshadowings of this expansive good news where 'nations will come to your light'– the 'nations' always being understood as the gentiles. 'The wealth of the nations will come to you', 'they shall bring gold and incense and they shall proclaim the praise of the LORD'. The presence of the magi heralds the arrival of some seriously dodgy people with the wrong credentials at the heart of God's good news.

But let's be clear – this visitation is not merely a manifestation of personal devotion, a sort of proto-interfaith expression of shared spirituality: it is a very political moment. Matthew has already set his stall out with regard to the credentials of Jesus: he is in the line of King David; Joseph, his father, is addressed as 'son of David'; and the political and spiritual hopes of a nation are invested in his opening rollcall of names that go back to Abraham, all culminating in the birth of this baby boy in Bethlehem. The magi naively and clumsily inquire concerning the whereabouts of the 'king of the Jews', to the existing king of the Jews, Herod. At the close of Matthew's Gospel, we will be participants to a big question about who is *really* in charge when Jesus is brought before the High Priest and Pontius Pilate at his trial. So at his birth, amid a constellation of King Herod and strange visitors from the East with their royal gifts, kingship is subverted and reimagined. The inescapable context of the birth of Jesus is a *Game of Thrones* saga where this Bethlehem baby fulfils the hopes of Israel to the reign of God among them and displaces all current powers. Worship of this baby king in a manger will have repercussions that challenge authorities and break across cultural and religious divides.

What we have here in this strange visitation is God at work revealing himself in the birth of Jesus and interrupting the powers that be in ways that demand a questioning of all that we hold dear. Mysteriously and provocatively, God speaks to these dodgy astrologers in ways that are understandable to them. We have no idea where this leads; what conversion or discipleship outcomes will ensue. All we know is that Jesus is central to this story and that there is an irresistible opening up of this good news to all sorts of people.

We may well ask again 'What was that all about?' as we move into the New Year with our tattered resolutions and our struggling fitness and diet regimes. We are not the only ones to be blinking from the arrival of multiple visitors and their inappropriate gifts. I suspect just like the Holy Family, we would ponder the cosmic mystery of God come among us in the birth of Jesus, with all our hopes set in him. But as we ponder this mystery, we would also see the troubling upsetting of expectations and allegiances and the messiness of seeing surprising guests at the party.

4

Attending to the Eloquent Body: Lancelot Andrewes and the Word

JESSICA MARTIN

Preaching is not really for the page. Its words are intended to be spoken in a time and a place, to a particular group of people who hear them at that moment and no other moment of their own lived experience. The textual forms of sermons are always a flattened copy of their embodied reality, as a play's script is only the 2D diagram of a theatrical experience.

This chapter attempts an impossible task: to convey something of the unique slice of time, space and shared experience that is a sermon. It therefore preserves its own original performance as a talk in a particular time and place. The matter of the talk itself is entirely focused on the relationship in preaching between written and spoken, read and acted, embodied and imagined. Once, what you read here was a talk given at Southwark Cathedral in 2014 to mark the day of the great preacher Lancelot Andrewes' death 388 years earlier. Here, you catch its echo; and (by the grace of God) his.

In the generation to which Lancelot Andrewes belonged, the spoken word had a life of its own. People flocked to sermons and to lectures as forms of grand entertainment; and although the spoken occasion might find a textual form afterwards, when it appeared in print, that printed form was often thought of as preserving the breathing, living form of the words as they had been performed before a live audience. A rough parallel, only slightly dated, would be between the experience of going to a live gig and buying the recorded version of the same songs. One copied the other, but no discerning person would think of them as being at all the same thing.

I can't offer grand entertainment, nor am I brave or silly enough to attempt to perform a memorized script for you this afternoon, as Andrewes and his contemporaries would have done when preaching. But in one respect this afternoon's lecture will follow the protocol of seventeenth-century spoken entertainment: there is nothing for you to look at. No PowerPoint, no pictures, no handouts. Only bodies and words in a room together, speaking and hearing. Andrewes' own highly characteristic form of preaching recognized that hearers (who might also be note-takers) needed clear divisions for their text, and short, pithy phrases to ponder, or they would get lost. His eloquence was designed for speech as much or more than it was made for the printed page. It seems fitting, therefore, for me to try to replicate – not his eloquence – but at least the conditions of his eloquence in this room this afternoon, by giving you an auditory experience unmediated through any visual aids. You have nothing to hold in your hands today.

Lancelot Andrewes, to whom T. S. Eliot ascribed a profound part in the shaping of the Church of England, died in Southwark on September 25 1626; his body was buried in this cathedral, then the parish church of St Saviour's, Southwark, about six weeks later, on 11 November. At his funeral, the preacher, John Buckeridge, described his death as a kind of speech-act, a final eloquence comparable or even equal to the achievements of his life, in these striking words:

> … now I applye my selfe and my Text, to the present Text, that lies before us … a man whose worth may not be passed over in silence, whom all ages with us may celebrate and admire … of whom I can say nothing … Heere I desire neither the tongue of man, nor Angells: if it were lawfull, I should wish no other but

> his own tongue and pen … let him speak of himselfe, none so fit as himselfe was, of whom I am to speake this day … And he now speakes. He speakes in his *learned Workes*, and *Sermons,* and he speakes in his *life* and *workes of mercy*, and he speakes in his *death*: and what he taught in his life and works, he taught and expressed in his death. He is the great *Actor* and *Performer*, I but the poore crier, *Vox clamantis*, He was the *Vox clamans*: he was the loud and great *crying Voice,* I am but the poore *Eccho*: and it is well with me, if as an *Eccho*, of his large and learned bookes and workes, I onely repeate a few of the last words.

Buckeridge uses here a frequent funeral technique of the time, where the preacher pointed to the silent eloquence of the coffin to preach mortality to the living auditors. You need to imagine such a coffin – lead-lined, one presumes, in Andrewes' case, given the time lapse between his death and his burial – displayed prominently before the congregation below the pulpit. It would be draped in black cloth; often the cloth would be pinned all over with the manuscript verse elegies of mourners, elegies that might find themselves reproduced at the front of commemorative volumes months – or perhaps years – later.

For a writer and preacher such as Andrewes the eloquent text of a dead body suffered the sea-change to a proclamation of resurrection almost more quickly and easily, in the circumstances, than his body could decay into its component parts of earth. Because, in that age of the rise of print, when the word spoken and written was prized almost more than any of the other works a priest could perform, a dead body became a living voice through reproduction, '*Eccho*': 'he was the loud and great *crying Voice*', preached Buckeridge, 'I am but the poore *Eccho*'. It was a commonplace that the dead spoke: a favourite preaching text was from the letter to the Hebrews, 11. 4, where the body of Abel, the first man to die, showed a faith 'dead yet speaking'. Even allowing for the huge popularity of sermons in the period as a form of performed mass entertainment (those were the days …), the dead spoke, potentially, to a lot more people and in a much more stable form – the printed text – than they had done in their performed sermons when living. The published works of preachers became emblems of their immortality under God, held between calf-bound covers; but that immortality could only be reached by traversing the deep waters of death. A popular frontispiece of the time shows a skeleton lying on a slab; a speech bubble emerges from the grinning mouth, which says '*mors ultima linea rerum est*' – 'Death is the last line – or perhaps the last utterance – of [all] things.' On either side of the slab rise stone columns supporting a roof made entirely of books.[56]

So when Buckeridge characterizes himself as a kind of fragmented ventriloquist for a life – Andrewes' life – where action and utterance merge, and where both action and utterance meet their ultimate meaning in a speaking death – he is doing nothing very unusual. Many were commemorated in this way, so many that the move was pretty much a cliché. But in Andrewes' particular case it was also unusually apt. Because Andrewes was someone for whom words and things, utterances and acts, were companions so close as to be joined. Not *the same* – there was a notional gap between them to be considered deeply. Just as humanity was separated from God, so words were separated from things, and could not always express entirely the things they represented. But, all the same, words and things were joined. For Andrewes, every word had its strong performative edge.

So here is Andrewes showing what that means, in a beatitude based upon the words of the epistle of James: 'be ye doers of the word, and not hearers only'. In Andrewes' rendition it becomes this: 'Blessed are they, that so incarnate the written word, by doing it, as the Blessed Virgin gave flesh, to the aeternall Word, by bearing it.'

---

56 Thomas Fuller, *Abel Redevivus or the dead yet speaking; the lives and deaths of the moderne divines* (London, 1651).

So – just in case anyone thinks preaching has relatively little to do with life – here's a challenge: as you read the word of God, the Scriptures of the Old and New Testaments that contain the good news of Jesus, you *enflesh* the gospel, you *incarnate* it, in doing so. Your process is a kind of mirror image, reversed image, of what happened to that other word, the Word made flesh, when God became a human body enclosed in the womb of a young woman, and was born into a fragile body that as yet knew no words: the Word without a word. The paradox of God as a speechless infant is one that Andrewes dwells on tenderly in several sermons. Mary bears a bodily Word, becomes *theotokos*, God-bearer; we bear the good news in our bodies in being and action. Gradually, speaking and experience come close enough to touch.

This is a tremendously hopeful understanding of our human relationship to God. Simply in the act of reading the Scriptures we are invited to experience salvation, here and now, in a kind of participatory action with God's creative speech. 'Let there be light' can fill our bodies full of light. Andrewes had little time for the anxious, endless debate on predestination that preoccupied so many of his contemporaries: he is quite sure that it is given to human beings to choose to align themselves with the actions of God. Incarnation happens all the time, he says; it happens now; and here. Famously, he took the example of Lot's wife to illustrate what he thought about human choice and will: she was not predestined to look back upon the city of destruction, but chose to do so. She turned away from God; by the same token, to turn the other way, to turn towards the actions of God in the world, people embraced salvation.

For once a year (writes Andrewes, in a sermon preached in the springtime, at Lent) all things turn. And that once is now at this time, for now at this time is the turning of the year. In heaven, the sun in his equinoctial line, the zodiac and all the constellations in it, do now turn about to the first point. The earth and all her plants, after a dead winter, return to the first and best season of the year. The creatures, the fowls of the air, the swallow and the turtle, and the crane and the stork, know their seasons, and make their just return at this time every year. Everything now turning that we also would make it our time to turn to God in.

Andrewes puts in his echoes of the great biblical love song, the Song of Songs ('the swallow and the turtle [dove] are heard in our land'), as part of a great and deliberate celebration of meeting God this moment, in passionate immediacy. The spring of life, he says, is this now, right now, this very raw seventeenth-century London spring. Andrewes' own understanding of the cyclical time of the church year brings multiple *nows* together at the appointed times of year. Every Christmas God is borne in and from the body of Mary and the word cries wordlessly into the hearts of his human creatures. Every Lent the world turns, inviting us to turn with it, to repent, turn back to the passion of God's love. Every Easter death suffers its sea-change to new life. It is not symbolic recall. Now means now – and Andrewes uses the words *now*, *here* absolutely performatively, to bring the scriptural moment and the time of our lives together, to *incarnate* the word in doing and speaking, until doing and speaking merge into passionate experience.

Here is the most extraordinary of those moments, at the crown of Andrewes' perception of the actions of God. It is one where, like Buckeridge, I can only be a 'poor *Eccho*', attempting a rehearsal, a repetition, of a moment almost 300 years old which is *at the same time* the now of today, 27th September 2014 – and a moment in a garden 2,000 years ago. Three nows, all adjoining and joining.

Here is the text from the Gospel of John: 'Jesus saith to her, Mary: She turned her selfe, & said to Him, Rabboni: that is to say Master.'

This is the recognition in the garden between Mary and the risen Christ, invoked by Andrewes in his Easter sermon of 1620, and it sounds like this:

> Now *magnus amoris amor.* Nothing so allures, so drawes love to it, as doth love it selfe. In *Christ* specially, and in such in whom the same minde is. For, when *her Lord saw*, there was no taking away *His taking away* from her, all was in vaine, neither men nor *Angels*, nor *Himselfe* (so long as he kept *Himselfe gardiner*) could get any thing of her, but *her Lord* was gone, *He was taken away*; and that for want of *Jesus*, nothing but *Jesus* could yield her any comfort; *Hee* is no longer able to containe, but even discloses *Himselfe*; and discloses *Himselfe* by *His* voice.
>
> For, it should seeme, before, with His shape, Hee had changed that also. But now, he speakes to her in *His* knowen voice, in the wonted accent of it, does but name her name, *Mary*, no more, and that was enough...
>
> And now, loe, *Christ* is found, found alive that was sought dead. A cloude may be so thick, we shall not see the Sunne through it. The Sunne must scatter that cloud, and then wee may. Here is an example of it. It is strange, a thick cloude of heavinesse had so covered her, as, see *Him* she could not, through it: this one word, these two syllables, [*Mary*] from *His* mouth, scatters it, all. So sooner had *His* voice sounded in her ears, but it drives away all the mist, dries up her teares, lightens her eyes, that she knew *Him* straight, and answeres *Him* with her wonted salutation, *Rabboni.* If it had been in her power to have raised *Him* from the dead, shee would not have failed, but done it (I dare say). Now it is done to her hands.

And, with this, all is turned out and in. A new world, now.

Well. Is this remembering, or re-enacting, or simply being present in the Easter recognition? It is all of these, at once. For *now* and *here* to align like this, to make new worlds join with the old, Andrewes must have a high view of memory. And he does. The Lot's wife sermon I was talking about has the shortest of texts, 'Remember Lot's wife', given both in English and in Latin as *Memore estote Uxoris Lot*. Andrewes has a lot of fun with the Latin imperative for 'remember': *memore*. Yes, it is a cross-lingual pun of the kind he enjoys so much, and an easy one to make since the two words share an etymology, but Andrewes is not just having fun. If the command to remember and the English word 'memory' are homophones, that is not blind chance but a sign, a message, that human memory has its roots in the divine command to remember. We remember the word of Scripture, and we remember the Divine Word who came into the world, because that is what memory is for.

It will come as no surprise that Andrewes' understanding of memory is sacramental: the *anamnesis*, the not-forgetting of the act of Communion is at the heart of sacred memory. Andrewes' Hebraic knowledge will also recall that the act of remembering in biblical texts is does not mean the act of synthetic recall implied by the English word – it is perhaps unavoidable that our modern sensibilities will reach for the superficial analogies of digital visual record, the automatic replays of the recording machine. That is not what is meant by biblical remembering. Instead, it is an act which re-members – which brings into the present, through deep immersion and symbolic re-presentation, the events that are its substance. To remember Christ's sacrifice is to bring the single moment of bodily giving into the present. It isn't a repetition. It's not that there were lots of moments of breaking and giving away. There was one moment, but it remains present through all time; and in the Sacrament its continual present-ness is recalled, made concrete. Andrewes had quite a lot of time for the doctrine of transubstantiation, considering how unpopular it was in the Protestant English devotional imagination; but it seems to me that he would not have made all that much distinction, essentially, between it and memorialist understandings of the sacrament of the most uncompromising kind. The command to remember is consonant with the command to do the gospel in the act of reading, to incarnate God's salvation.

Andrewes preached on the sacrament of Holy Communion in the year 1598, taking as his text Isaiah 6.6-7, the moment where the prophet's sins are taken away by the action of a seraph who touches his tongue with a live coal. Often invoked as a symbol for preaching the gospel (and used in one common blessing for deacons before the gospel is proclaimed), Andrewes sees it as the moment when the wine touches the communicant's lips. For him, it is a Eucharistic image.

'And here we have matter offered us of faith' he preaches:

> that as [God] ... used the touching of a cole, to assure the Prophet that his sinnes were taken away; so in the Sacrament he doth so elevate a piece of bread, and a little wine, and make them of such power; that they are able to take away our sinnes: And this maketh for Gods glory, not only to beleeve that God can work our Salvation, without any outward means, but by the inward Grace of his Spirit; but also, that he can elevate the meanest of his creatures; not onlye the hemme of a garment, but even a strawe, (if he see it good) shall be powerfull enough, to save us from our sinnes. As Christ himself is spirituall and bodily; so he taketh away our sinnes, by means not only spiritual but bodily; as in the Sacrament.[57]

For Andrewes the physicality of the Sacrament, the real presence of bread and wine as they touch the lips, is a necessary corollary to the real-ness of Christ in his incarnation as well as in his coming in the Spirit as it is manifested in the written word of the Scriptures and upon the fleshy tables of the heart. Such a concentration upon the immediacy of the bodily action also offers some way of understanding what the Sacrament might be to those of failing or destroyed memory, a preoccupation for any priest who brings home Communion to those with dementia or stroke or other injuries and violences of the brain. If it is not vital to recall the mental event, but only essential to participate in the physicality of the act, then the experience of Communion is the one thing necessary.

---

57 Lancelot Andrewes, in Peter McCullough (ed.), *Selected Sermons and Lectures* (Oxford: OUP 2005), p. 143.

Andrewes brings the same immediacy to his understanding of what it is to look upon God. This was a really problematic area for Protestant London at that time, and especially in relation to the most essential devotional act of beholding: that of regarding Christ upon the cross. The generations of pre-Reformation 'beholding' around the Passion narrative, the emotively realized details of Christ's sufferings from Gethsemane to Calvary, made this a dangerous area for reformed sensibilities. You find the martyrologist John Foxe, preaching on Good Friday in London in 1570, replacing the potentially idolatrous image of Christ's physical body on the cross with a legal text taken from Paul's letter to the Colossians:

> And here now havyng taken downe the crucified body of Jesus from the Crosse, to occupy your eyes, and to delite your myndes, I entend by the grace of Christ crucified, to set up here … a new Roode unto you, a Crucifixe that may do all Christen hartes good to behold. This Crucifixe is hee that crucified all mankynde … his name is the lawe of commaundements … wherof ye shall heare what S. Paule speaketh … *This law* (saieth he) *of commaundementes, or Gods handwrytyng that was agaynst us in decrees, hee hath made voyde, abolished, and hath affixed to his crosse, and spoyling principates and potestates, hath made an open shew of them, triumphyng over them openly in him selfe, Col.2.* And thus have ye upon one Crosse ii.(two) crucifixes, ii. most excellent potentates, that ever were, the sonne of God, and the law of God, wrastlyng together about mans salvation, both cast downe & both slayne upon one Crosse …[58]

This is an incredibly corkscrew way of trying to ensure that the Pauline epistles of salvation trump the emotional effect of pre-reformed devotion to the cross of Christ. Barely 30 years later, Andrewes completely ignores all such reformed anxieties. For him, the act of beholding and the act of reading are so folded together

58 Foxe, *Good Friday 1570*, ff. 53r–54v.

as to be almost identical. Here he is preaching on the Zechariah text, 'They shall look upon him whom they have pierced', identified through its Johannine use as an allusion to the scene of Christ's crucifixion:

> There is no part of the whole course of our Saviour CHRIST's life or death, but it is well worthy our *looking on*; and from each part in it, there goeth vertue to do us good. But, of all other parts, and above them all, this last part, of his piercing, is commended unto our view … if there be any *grace* in us, we will thinke it worth the looking on. … for, at every looking, some new *sight* will offer it selfe, which will offer unto us occasion, either of godly *sorrow*, true *repentance*, sound *comfort*, or some other reflexion, issuing from the beames of this heavenly mirror … *looke and lamente* or *mourne*, which is indeed the most kindly and natural effect of such a spectacle. *Looke upon Him that is pierced*, and with *looking upon Him*, be *pierced* thy selfe: *Respice & transfigere.*[59]

To look is to be transfigured. In looking the beholder is changed by the sight of Christ into a new person, altered for ever by beholding a death into a site of new life. No need to go via the Pauline arguments for the liberating nature of salvation. We turn only to the sight of Christ dying at Golgotha: simpler, and infinitely harder than the 'wrastlyng' about the nature of law and grace preoccupying Foxe on his Good Friday meditation.

Harder, but absolutely hospitable. It is not necessary that you remember yourself and your own history in order to look upon God. When we are no longer able to remember for ourselves, the sacrifice of our Lord remembers for us: Jesus, remember me. As in the James Montgomery hymn based around the *anamnesis* of communion: 'this I will do, my dying Lord, I will remember thee'; we end without memory, and drifting, and rest upon God's own remembering of us:

59 McCullough (ed.), *Selected Sermons*, pp. 123, 131.

And when these failing lips grow dumb,
And mind and memory flee,
When thou shalt in thy kingdom come,
Jesu, remember me.[60]

In my end is my beginning. Today is the commemoration of a death, the death of Lancelot Andrewes 388 years ago. During the course of that summer of 1626 mind and memory withdrew, and finally breath and speech, leaving only the textual body of Andrewes' words, eloquent in death. In those words, echoed in fragments today, Andrewes' life of faith (he prayed for five hours daily) and the extraordinary integrity of his perception of God acting in the world, in the breath and bodies, the speech and looking of his human creatures, is vivified in our speaking and looking and thinking. Now; and here.

60 James Montgomery, 'According to thy gracious Word'.

The Passion of Remembering and Forgetting: Addresses for the Three Hours of Good Friday

JESSICA MARTIN

1st Address: The Scent of Water

Psalm 88.1–4; Job 14.1–14

> Why do you turn your eyes towards human suffering when you could enjoy the immeasurable prospect of your own endless being? If you fix your gaze upon mortals, all you will see is mortality.

This is the question Job asks his God. It's not a question about justice; Job makes no claim for fair treatment. He's thinking about something more fundamental than that. He is asking whether there can be any real relationship between beings so unlike as God and man: between the immortal judge and the living piece of ephemera that inhabits God's created world so faultily, so fleetingly. We can't even hold a conversation, says Job; how do we share the faculty of judgement, how can we begin to connect, let alone join, the way you and I see the world? You have all the power, all the life, all the goodness. You appoint stringent human limitations: people fade away into nothingness so quickly that to the immortal eye they are barely a stir in the dust. In what way, then, are we made in your image? What have we got even to talk about? Leave us alone.

There is no better time to ponder Job's question than on the day God dies – mortal, wounded, hated, abandoned. When he cries 'why hast thou forsaken me', whose voice may we hear? Is not Job's question somewhere in that cry? The covenant promise stands from Abraham onward: I AM with you. Job questions how that covenant may even be; and the fact of death is the main ground he offers for why it is impossible. How can the unclean, the fleeting, converse with the eternally pure? Jesus, the place where they meet, hangs now upon the cross; and his agony is that God is not there.

But he is there.

Job is a clever rhetorician. He is not really playing fair. He asks the question, for one thing – so he must be able at least to imagine the possibility of an answer. He is like the wounded partner in a married couple, announcing that the relationship is all broken in the hope that somehow saying so might impel the other one to fix it. His version of despair is actually a kind of hoping against hope. *Is this it?* Job asks, tacitly; *is death really all we've got? If we are going to vanish as if we had never been, what price your gaze upon us? Why did you bother to seduce us with your self? Should not immortal attention mean an immortal relationship for us both?*

Job has noticed that when you talk with God about death and life, mortality and immortality, then in relationship terms you are actually talking about forgetting and remembering. When the immortal gaze looks upon his creatures they are held in life, from moment to moment remembered. When it turns away they are – just not there. Not even dust. Mist, or smoke; less than a puff of air.

When God notices us, we thrive. Even as we suffer and die we are seen and known by the divine heart. If he were not to look our way we would not just be gone: we would be absolutely irrecoverable. All the many fleeting lives whose passionate relationships filled their own worlds: forgotten. The past like a waterfall dropping off the edge of the universe into nothing. Job rejects that thought. He turns to God as to a King in which all power is held, and he uses 'remember' as a formal term, as a way of describing how a King might reinstate a courtier fallen from favour, or a master issue manumission to a slave: 'appoint me a set time, and remember me'. His voice fills with longing: 'All the days of my service I would wait until my release should come'. 'Re-membering' is just what our English word says it is: it regenerates a lost being, re-makes a lost body. It brings us from nothingness into something. We re-emerge into the gaze of life.

Job, for all his sorrow, is toying with the idea that in God's sight there is more to life than death. He reaches for an image of water, because water is where life happens. Are we just gradually drying up, he asks, like a silting lake or a river in drought? Will we blow away on the viewless winds? Or do we share in the hope of a felled tree, 'that at the scent of water it will bud and put forth branches like a young plant'? If death is part of a cycle that leads again to life in God's countenance, he says, I can wait as long as it takes.

The 'scent of water' is a mysterious phrase, for water, like spring, has no scent. But the hidden working of new life, its possibility and promise, are vivid in it. Of all our senses, the sense of smell, unwilled, makes the vanished past present to us more powerfully than sight or hearing ever can. The smell of spring is a real thing, a curious mixture of grass and earth and rain and sun and the greening of trees. The smell of a running stream is different from the smell of a desert landscape. What we scent becomes our not-forgetting, the past recollected and lived in the mixture of present pain and joy that we call memory.

Below the barren ground the water is rising, a bare trickle; in the dry wood stirs the sap. Now it springs up; do you not perceive it? Where God dies, there the impossible relationship comes together as one: divine with human, eternity with time, the dying man with the living God. And through that dying man, our salvation, crying out in agony: 'My God, my God, why hast thou forsaken me?' Because his cry meets with no answer, we are put back into intimate conversation with the divine heart. We have been remembered, and are alive. We are held by the divine hand. At the scent of water we bud again, all because of the wood of this dry cross-tree.

> If mortals die, will they live again?
> All the days of my service I would wait
> until my release should come.[61]

2nd Address: Remembering

Psalm 88.5–8; Luke 22.14–21

When Jesus was born, before his retentive mind knew anything at all about how he was or what he was, before he possessed language or benefited from the way its structures fix the images of memory, before he knew who he belonged to or whether he was, or was not, his mother; before all those things, he was laid in a manger. He was heavenly food in a feeding trough. From his first breath, from before he knew as well as from after he learnt the stresses, the breaking points, of his earthly work, Jesus inhabited human time in order to be broken and given away, to be poured out like a libation or like a fountain soaking dry ground. Whole and pure, he came into being in order to be fragmented and scattered abroad. Emptying himself of power, he was handed, utterly vulnerable, into the love of a young girl; and into the marginal, often dangerous, family role of stepchild.

Now Jesus sits among those who love him. They are meeting to celebrate the Passover. They are bringing into the present moment a night when a lamb was ritually slaughtered in order to save the first-born of Israel, the beginning of the release of its people into freedom. The present into which their remembering brings that story is a difficult one, for again the people of Israel are possessed by a foreign power. At Passover the people dream dangerous dreams of freedom and of violence, and the streets are uneasy. 'I have eagerly desired to eat this Passover with you', says Jesus.

61 Job 14.14.

But then he interrupts himself. He sets himself aside from the group of men and women sharing their story of liberation. Whatever part he must play in the unfolding purpose of the Exodus story, it is neither that of the freed slave nor that of the prophetic leader. He says, with sudden, unnerving detachment, offering the cup of wine: 'Take it and divide it among yourselves'. The nourishment he offers is not, after all, going to nourish him. 'From now on I will not drink of the fruit of the vine until the kingdom of God comes'. He speaks like one who is already cut off from the living; he speaks like the sacrificial Lamb. Past and future merge and flow together in the charged present of the shared sacred meal: 'I have eagerly desired to eat … I will not eat until the kingdom of God comes'. 'Take [the cup] … from now on I will not drink … until the kingdom of God comes'. The prayer he offers as he takes and breaks the bread offers himself, again and always, as food: 'This is my body, which is given for you'. In the fragments torn from the warm loaf dwells every moment of given-away life, from the overshadowing of his conception to the last breath his words look towards, every act, every word, every healing touch, every sign of God's life working to renew the weary, bad, dying world.

Then he looks at his friends, and offers a new and even more riskily fragile token of love. He asks them for something. Even as the shadow of isolated suffering that is to come draws him away from the warm circle of the living, he speaks longingly, as the dead might speak, calling out of Sheol into the dreams of the living.

He says, *remember me.*

Job noticed that we live and flourish when God remembers us. But what does it mean when God asks us to remember him? What can our mayfly eyes and minds, our unstable and betraying hearts, possibly offer God? It is not for us to open the prison in which the dead are shut up, or to grant God manumission.

The world is full of people for whom we can do nothing.

Many are dead – those we have loved and for whom we grieve, or strangers (now or in the past) whose stories make us weep uselessly. There are those who are alive but who are imprisoned in different ways: some with walls and bars, or with arbitrary exclusions from those good things necessary to life. Others are imprisoned in bodily miseries, through stroke or other injury to body or brain; for others the pathways for the faculty of memory degenerate, leaving them progressively more unknown to themselves. What price remembering for those who suffer so cruel a diminution? Why visit someone who will not recall a day later that you ever came?

And we can do nothing for Jesus, as he looks towards his own slow breaking. But last requests are sacred, and the unwilled responses that love makes don't calculate how useful something will be, or even if it will be useful at all. If our dying Lord says *remember me*, then we will remember. Like the women standing far off and watching him die, even if we cannot alleviate his suffering we can hold him in our gaze, and when we do that for him, every isolated and suffering person there ever has been or will be is remembered with him and heaven hears us saying, *you are part of us. You are not alone.* Intercessory prayer is the work of remembering the whole body of God's children, but especially those who are forgotten by the world or who can no longer remember themselves. Cicero said of crucified criminals that they should not even be had in mind. Jesus asks us to ignore such brutal fastidiousness, and to remember.

Jesus is not only asking for our remembrance. He asks it in a context that brings the past into the present, where the signs of remembrance become the continuing actions of Christ's sustaining life. 'Do this' he says, and again the little word 'this' re-enacts the whole world of Christ's life from its first beginnings to its ending on this day. We remember him not only in our hearts but in our bodies, the Word of God burgeoning in the remembrance of his children – not just in sharing bread and wine but in every act following our sending out into the world, the broken fragments of the Body of Christ feeding the world soul by soul, each one both whole in itself and a fragment of the larger whole that is the community of Christ's spiritual siblings.

John Donne, writing meditations upon the prison of human isolation, once famously said 'Every man's death diminishes me'. But I tell you that the other side of that is that every act of remembering – whether of the dead or of the lost living – participates in the living gaze of God, holding those we love within life, making them present in a community of love that brings the past, living and active, into the present and gives it into the loving purposes of the eternal now. We are called as servants to kneel and wash our neighbour, so that the scent of water might bring the living sap rising through feet distorted by the weight of time upon them. This is how we give ourselves away to those who have, through sorrow, misfortune or damage, forgotten what it was to be themselves, who are cut off from their own stories.

And the day I falter and forget my history and my purpose, lost in the labyrinths of my own damaged brain, the remembering of the rest of the Body of Christ shall, by grace, carry me towards life.

While we can, we will remember Christ, and, when at the last we fall into forgetting, he will remember us.

3rd Address: What shall I cry?

Psalm 88.9–12; Isaiah 40.6–11

Do you remember, when you were little, what it was like to have a sheet of blank paper in front of you that you planned to fill with something wonderful? Perhaps a story – just the right shape, not tailing off when the plot got out of control or full of unintended diversions; perhaps a picture, with the proportion and perspective correct for once and the colour laid on evenly, with a subtlety you can in fact never really get from felt pens. The longing to begin, its sense of possibility, was one of the purest pleasures of my own childhood; and though nothing I wrote ever lived up to the joy of wanting to, I was not deterred. I could hear the voice saying 'Cry out!' with beautiful clearness and was confident that in the rushes and flashes of constant lived experience there was so very much I could say in answer to its invitation. I didn't have much technical skill to worry about, because I hadn't mastered much, and the process of turning experience from something fleeting into something fixed and unfading looked as if it would be easy. Even now, deep down, on the other side of discovering just how impossible, partial and fragmentary this whole business of using language is, I still have an irrational belief that the truth of experience can be spoken in all its complexity if I just concentrate well enough on what needs to be said.

The speaker in Isaiah is young enough to hear the voice's invitation, and old enough to know that there are few unfading words. In the constant slippage of mortal living the words we speak, even those we manage to record in some stable form, suffer their sea-changes in the flow of time, becoming something we never quite meant or slipping out of meaning altogether. The Scripture writer, whose name is probably not Isaiah and whose writing was intended for another context than ours, begins to wonder whether time's slippages mean that nothing can really be said of the eternal – nothing except how implacably its presence reveals us to be ephemeral.

But then he changes his mind. From the very slippages and shifts, the decays and mutations of what can be said, from the depredations of time itself, God speaks, transforming each small death of meaning, each lost bit of story, into something richer and stranger than our limited intention can imagine, pointing onwards at mystery. 'The grass withers, the flower fades, but the word of our God will stand for ever' (Isaiah 40.8). The eternal continually breaks into the flow of time and touches its creatures with unexpected, unlooked-for blessing.

Once upon a time the Word of God was expressed as a

single human life, the life of Jesus. In this man, named after salvation and heralded with bright, mysterious signs, that Word appeared. It was perishable as flesh and slippery as blood. He told us he brought good news. He cherished the poor and valued the marginal, healed the sick and rebuked the powerful. In him the Kingdom of God came near, lighting up the fleeting world. These things happened, and their meanings transform our living.

In him this day, the day of his death, the Word of God is wounded, destroyed, silenced. His love becomes love unknown. He joins the swift passage of human ephemera obliterated by circumstances, lost among the dead, lost with all the rest of us, beyond praise and longing and prayer, beyond righteousness and remembrance, beyond any of the meanings of breathing, thinking, feeling life. In his acts, unrecorded in his lifetime, in his obscure death, eternity writes its messages in dust.

But still we hear them. We remember that the eternal Word of God visits and redeems the forgotten bodies of the innumerable dead and raises them up to praise.

> Get you up to a high mountain,
> O Zion, herald of good tidings;
> lift up your voice with strength,
> O Jerusalem, herald of good tidings,
> lift it up, do not fear;
> say to the cities of Judah,
> 'Here is your God!'[62]

4th Address: Forgetting

Psalm 38.6–11; Luke 22.39–46

We remember our lives in a story-shaped way. We order our lives into story through the structures of language, and especially those that mark the passing of time. It may be that the material we

62 Isaiah 40.9.

are ordering appears to us more like a series of mental pictures, but they are slotted into adjacent frames and joined together by explaining what came before what, or how that picture was altered or enriched or even cancelled by some other more significant picture.

And once we have that framework, we will also find ourselves deciding that this or that detail, this or that scene or moment, does not belong. Human beings are as much editors as they are makers. As soon as you set up as a storyteller, your memories settle around that story's shape. The memory becomes the story, and in order that one kind of memory may be preserved you will have to set about some deliberate forgetting. Then, after a while, you may find that your deliberate forgetting has become actual forgetting; your story structure has become so powerful that the things that don't fit fall away altogether. Forgetting is necessary to the process of remembering, always. The most powerful element in ordering memory is the kind of story you have decided to tell.

Much of what we forget is stuff that doesn't matter. You will not be particularly diminished if you can't remember what you had for dinner on March 25th two years ago. But people edit other stuff into forgetting besides the trivial. What about the experience you cannot bear to look at, the possibility you can't bring yourself to contemplate, the telling detail or event that shows you that the person you love most has begun to slip out of recognition, the painful scene that tears at your heart so deeply that you excise it altogether in order to protect yourself against the experience of constant pain? These are also the stuff of forgetting, and although they are often merciful they are all signs of our spiritual fragility, of our eye-blink refusals to participate in God's work of remembering from the depths to the heights of human experience, from the meaningless to the most charged of our utterances, acts and moments. We are too frail, and we cannot do it.

'Pray that you do not come into the time of trial!' Jesus says to his companions. He does not ask them to pray for him. He looks at their vulnerability and he removes himself and his agony from their direct sight; when he speaks to them he suggests that they pray for deliverance from the traumas that may distort or break them, may make them unrecognizable to themselves, through fear or pain, torture or failure. Death is very terrible, but more terrible is the trial of contemplating the means, the time, the prospect of extinction; more terrible is alienation, isolation, hatred, becoming less than human in the sight of another's eyes. These are the trials from which we pray to be released every time we pray the Lord's Prayer; and they are not good things, not character-building things. They are the terrible possibilities of every human life, and they break spirits before they break bodies. At the point where Jesus' own spirit bends and groans under the weight of the future, at the point where he looks at the breaking of his own body and the burden of hatred he will carry to his cross, he thinks only, and tenderly, of the needs of his friends, and offers them the sovereign remedy: prayer. *Pray that you may not come into the time of trial.*

Jesus is already there.

And Jesus' disciples know it. They don't sleep just because it happens to be late at night. They sleep 'because of grief'. Even though Jesus, in compassion, removes himself from their immediate sight, they know what is happening and they can't bear to look, can't bear even to think, what it might be to face towards the whole world's grief and carry it until, slowly and bit by bit, it destroys you. That is the cup that Jesus will drink, the cup that he asks his Father to spare him, if possible. And his friends' spirits cannot contemplate it. They go to sleep. They forget.

Imagine, now, that all the things that our self-protective spirits have slept through are regarded by that compassionate eye, now in the agony in the garden. The stuff that does not fit the seemliness of public stories. You do not have to go far afield, or search for the too-visible sufferings of the wider world. You will not have to travel more than a mile or two from where we are sitting now. Somewhere close under the lee of this cathedral church someone has been told they are going to die; is walking through the severe discipline of learning to let go of child, spouse, parent, the bright hopes of future actions, future making and doing and being.

Someone else nearby is leaning forward to speak to the person they are closest to in the world, when they discover that the words they imagined they said have come out as nonsense, and the troubled smile on their beloved's face tells them that they are shut out from the joy of conversing, now and for ever. They will, perhaps, remember that this has happened before, over and over, and that they themselves keep forgetting how impossible communication is, that their real and present grief is warded away by their beloved companion, who cannot bear to experience it daily, and so both forget, are complicit in forgetting, day after day, that they are cut away from each other, that the bridge of shared language is down and will never be rebuilt.

In a nearby hospital there will be people calling out for parents long dead, wandering on hiking trails that disappeared 40 years ago, fighting wars long over. Someone is trapped in a temporal loop in the brain that brings up, over and over again, a terrible event as if for the first time, and those who stand by hear only the continual crying and shut it out as best they can.

Someone in a place near here has won a victory against a destructive habit that is killing them, and knows already that the victory is so temporary as to be invisible. Someone in a place near here has tried to make a cup of tea and has lost the names of all the utensils, the algorithm of what must be done with cup and teabag and spoon, and stands wondering at the meaningless shapes on the once-familiar tabletop. Someone near here endures patiently the impersonal care of men and women who assume she understands nothing, and that the words she speaks – however passionate, however deeply meant – must therefore be discounted, weightless. She might have no voice at all. Worst of all, she understands that sometimes – but not always – they are right. When she dies, her patience and self-restraint will disappear out of her told story: 'at the end she was away with the fairies, poor darling'. No one will know what a hero she was, or the number of times she had to forgive her neighbour.

In the agony in the garden, Jesus is sustained by angels. Part of that sustenance is the tears wept for him by the woman who saw his sorrow and was courageous enough to meet it with her own, wiping them away with her hair. Do not always forget, try to remember when you can.

Beside him Jesus' friends absent themselves because of grief. But as they, and we, sleep, the Lord of life drops tears of blood for the forgotten sorrows of the whole world.

5th Address: Pools of water

Psalm 38.13–15; Isaiah 41.17–20

We live when our God remembers us, because in his presence is life. But not all remembering brings life, and not all forgetting is destruction.

When Judas betrayed his Lord to death, his acts and their consequences were pressed upon him so continually that he could not support his existence. He said to the elders, as it is told in the Gospel of Matthew, 'I have sinned by betraying innocent blood', and he attempted to give back the guilt with the blood money: thirty pieces of silver. Thirty pieces of silver is the amount that the book of Exodus gives as the price for the accidental death of a slave. The elders refused the responsibility by refusing the money, and Judas was driven to throwing it upon the ground because no one would receive it.

He was in a state of mind where no mercy of forgetting

was possible. No ritual act would empty his mind of what he had done, neither the acknowledgement of his sin, nor of his victim's innocence, nor the restitution of the derisory sum of money he had agreed to receive. None of this undid what had happened. It filled the foreground of his thoughts and pressed upon his chest on awaking. Memory became present torment, and forgetfulness a final good he most desperately sought. He looked for death as one who seeks the relief of being nothing at all. His life had become bent around this one act, the act for which he is remembered, when he pursued the betrayal of his Lord in a spirit of contempt, and brought it to fruition in a kiss, mimicking the gestures of love in the service of hatred. Allowing himself to be possessed by evil, he discovered himself to be more absolutely enslaved than he could possibly have imagined.

Although human beings must shoulder the interim judgements of life spent in community together, it is not given to us, thank God, to usurp the final divine judgement of any other person whatsoever. And today of all days is not one for pronouncing human judgement, for that would shout down the prayer our Lord offers for his killers as he is dying: 'Father, forgive them, for they do not know what they are doing'. One of the enduring characteristics of sin is to become unknown to oneself, unrecognizable in one's own acts and thoughts. Even Judas may have imagined that he was doing something quite other; he may have imagined that he was saving the lives of Jesus' companions, or averting a major incident, by offering the authorities a single ringleader. Or he may not have thought at all, driven by extremes of feeling. We do not know.

In contemplating the tragedy of Jesus' death our office is to recognize ourselves in every one of the players. The torments of guilt following an irreversible act of betrayal are not unique to Judas; nor is the despairing desire to be made nothing, the sense that death might be the only cleansing act of forgetting that is left. These are real and bitter parts of universal human experience, for which there is nothing to be done but to throw ourselves upon the mercy of God.

Yet when all we can do is to remember, it is the mercy of God to forget – if we will allow him. Beyond the stony ground of tragedy and its consequences lies an unimaginable compassion. 'I, I am He who blots out your transgressions for my own sake, and I will not remember your sins' (Isaiah 43.25).

There is no reason for God's mercy; it is not part of the logic of human acts and their outworkings. It is a pure gift, offered for the sake of his loving being. It is a fountain of water in the desert, springing up to heal and restore the parched and thirsty soul. It is the baptismal flood that invites us to leave sorrow behind, forgotten, dissolved into the saving water, through which, by the grace of God and the life and death of Jesus Christ, we may be reborn, restored, freed from the barren torments of memory into fruitful living. For even in the vale of misery *the pools are full of water* (Psalm 84.6).

God dies now before our eyes stretched upon a cross of dry, dead wood. Yet rivers of mercy flow down from it; and the ground upon which they fall is transformed from a barren waste to a land full of living and gracious trees:

> I will put in the wilderness the cedar,
> the acacia, the myrtle, and the olive;
> I will set in the desert the cypress,
> the plane and the pine together,
> so that all may see and know,
> all may consider and understand,
> that the hand of the LORD has done this.[63]

63 Isaiah 41.19-20 .

6th Address: The passion of remembering and forgetting

Psalm 31.13–14; Luke 22.54–62

'Simon, Simon, listen! Satan has demanded to sift all of you like wheat, but I have prayed for you that your faith will not fail; and you, when once you have turned back, strengthen your brothers.' These are Jesus' words to Peter at the Last Supper as Luke tells it, before the Gethsemane vigil and Jesus' arrest. Peter's response is characteristically impulsive, instinctively loyal: 'Lord, I am ready to go with you to prison and to death!' But Jesus knows that Peter's are words of the moment, part of the grandstanding of love. They have not counted the cost or truly faced the prospect they gesture towards. Yet they are generous, even if they are the largesse of a debtor. Jesus sees both their virtue and their inadequacy, though he can't fail to notice that Peter has missed his point. And that's not surprising; Jesus is trying to give his friend hope and strength to sustain him beyond a failure that hasn't happened yet.

We have just heard that failure happen. Peter, faithful enough to follow his Lord to the gate of his temporary prison, does not find the courage, in the dark hours just before dawn, to affirm his love and loyalty. His rejection deliberately widens the gulf between the imprisoned Jesus and his still-free companions; although the trial is still to come, we are aware from this moment that Jesus is a dead man walking, cut off from the living: *they of mine acquaintance were afraid of me; I am clean forgotten, as a dead man out of mind.*

Peter thrusts Jesus from his mind. He declares an absolute forgetting: *no, no, this relationship never existed at all.* As if a small god were to announce 'I do not remember you', and the creature so cursed were to become as if it had never been. Most mercifully, Peter is not God, and his terrified attempt to save himself by consigning his friend to oblivion has limited force. Jesus himself mends it, then and there, by refusing to disappear. He looks across the courtyard and meets his friend's eyes. This is not accusation. He does it to renew the relationship Peter's words have attempted to destroy. 'Then Peter remembered the word of the Lord, how he had said to him, "Before the cock crows today, you will deny me three times." And he went out and wept bitterly.'

Peter's tears are the pools of water in the dry ground of his betrayal. They are the way in which, in Jesus' words at supper the previous night, he 'turns back' from self-protective destruction. This 'turning back' is sometimes called 'repentance' – a specialist word that means 'turning back', or even '*metanoia*', a yet more specialist word that means 'absolute change' or 'reversal' – a transformative change of heart. Jesus' gaze upon Peter holds him in mind and recalls him to himself; God incarnate looks upon him and saves him from the torment of becoming lost, a stranger to his own heart. But it is Peter's tears, his *metanoia*, that water his renewal, his turning away from sin and towards life.

On the transformed other side of tragedy, Jesus and Peter will stand together again, a brazier of coals between them, and Peter will again be asked a question three times. Jesus will ask him, 'Do you love me?' And Peter will answer, 'Lord, you know everything; you know that I love you'. Jesus' response points him outwards: 'feed my lambs'. It's the same commission as the one he makes before Peter's betrayal: 'when once you have turned back, strengthen your brothers'. It's the same commission we also receive: re-member your love for me by carrying that love outwards. Give it to others. Carry it across the world. Remember that Christ looks out of the eyes of every condemned man and every rejected soul. Feed my lambs.

Here is the Passion of remembering and forgetting. We are remembered in God's sight, and we join ourselves to that life-giving memory when we remember Jesus, in his life, in his death, in his example taken, broken, blessed and given out to others in our lives and actions. The agony of our Lord remembers the sorrows we cannot contemplate and honours them in his own passion, alone in the garden. Last of all, he remembers us when we become lost and forgotten to ourselves, and in his loving gaze we are found again. When we cannot forget our sins he washes them away with life-giving water, until they are removed as far away from us as the east is from the west, until they are blotted out and utterly forgotten.

We will remember Jesus, on this day of all days, who dies upon the cross for our merciful forgetting.

We will remember Jesus, on this day of all days, who remembers us when we cannot.

We will remember Jesus, on this day of all days, in whose blessed death all our sins are forgotten.

We will remember Jesus.

5

Attending to the Word in Silence and Lectio Divina

SISTER JUDITH SLG

Your word is a lamp to my feet and a light to my path.
(Psalm 119.105)

When Charles de Foucauld spent hours meditating on the Scriptures in Nazareth he often heard Jesus say to him 'cry the Gospel from the rooftops, not with words but with your life' – words that he put into practice. This chapter explores the benefits of attending to the word in silence, as he did, as preparation, not only for preaching, but also for the listening that happens as we hear sermons. In a world where our attention is a scarce commodity that is so often the focus of aggressive digital marketing, the ability to train our attention becomes increasingly crucial. I explore how to spend time in prayer, how to listen to the word of God, in order to develop disciplines that not only help us in sermon preparation, as we turn to the task of committing words to paper or screen, but also our listening more generally, so that we may cry the gospel with our lives.

The contemplative community of which I am a member gives ample opportunity for this, with time set apart for silent prayer and Lectio Divina (or Holy Reading), in addition to the daily use of the psalms in the Offices. Plenty of opportunity to attend to the word in silence, but Lectio Divina doesn't necessarily make it any easier though.

I was struck at the beginning of our Easter Vigil this year by the sentence in the opening prayer that says, 'For this is the Passover of the Lord, in which through word and sacrament we share in his victory over death.' Our Vigil begins at 4.30 a.m. and I often anticipate with dread the seven long readings. This year I heard anew that one of the ways to share in Christ's victory over death is through the Word. I woke up to the need to attend to the word and asked myself, 'How can I best prepare myself really to hear it?'

The capital W is significant. 'The Word became flesh', as St John's Gospel tells us. When we read Scripture either alone or in the context of worship we are not simply reading. We enter into a personal relationship with a self-communicating God. A saying often attributed to St Jerome is, 'When you pray you speak to God, when you read Scripture God speaks to you.' It's easy to forget the reality of this, as I was in danger of doing at the Easter Vigil. The familiarity of the stories can dull the attention; or we can resist because we don't understand, or reject because the passage offends. Instead the question I need to ask myself is 'What is God saying to me? Today?' God is longing (for that is God's nature; God can do no other) to communicate with me. This is a dynamic relationship in which I can be confident that God is engaged. My part is to be fully attentive and present to God, listening in silence and expectation, with all my intelligence and faculties, to discern what God is saying as I am still and quiet, resting in God's presence. The dynamic relationship with the Word is based on the nature of God, not the skill of the pray-er. God finds a way around every barrier.

In 2009, at Magdala, excavations of the first-century synagogue revealed an intricately carved stone. The stone is thought to have housed the scrolls of the Torah. It is decorated, and one of the designs is a six-petalled flower that signals the presence of God. The juxtaposition of that design with the purpose of housing the text indicates that your fullest attention is required. It is saying, 'Here in the text is the Presence of God.' It asks for the patient practice of the disciplines of listening, so that we may be open to the infinitely rich treasure enclosed.

In 1991 Rowan Williams preached about reading the Bible.

He suggested that the best image we have for God's engagement with us through the biblical text is Jacob wrestling with the angel:

> Here in Scripture is God's urgency to communicate, here in scripture is our mishearing, misappropriating, our deafness and our resistance. Woven together in scripture are those two things, the giving of God and our inability to receive what God wants to give …[64]

Encounter, contest: perhaps when we read the words 'This text is being fulfilled today, even as you listen', we can say that that aspect of Scripture is being fulfilled in me now. In me now is God's gift, and in me now is the distorting glass of prejudice and fear. In me now the gift is being received. But the gift is also capable of being distorted and hemmed in, and not being given through me. All the complexity of the contesting of Scripture is in us as we listen to it. When we listen to a passage that is difficult, alien or offensive, I think our reaction should be neither to say 'This is the word of the Lord, so the difficulty is my problem', nor to say 'This is rubbish, we ought to produce a more politically correct version of Scripture!' Our task is rather to say that the revelation of God comes to us in the middle of weakness and fallibility. We read neither with a kind of blind and thoughtless obedience to every word of Scripture, as if it simply represented the mind of God, nor do we read with that rather priggish sensibility that desires to look down on the authors of Scripture as benighted savages. We read with a sense of our own benighted savagery in receiving God's gift, and our solidarity with those writers of Scripture caught up in the blazing fire of God's gift who yet struggle with it, misapprehend it and misread it.

This was a sermon that had a profound and lasting effect on my life, enabling and enriching my living of my Christian discipleship and relationship to God.

---

64 Rowan Williams, 'Reading the Bible', in *Open to Judgement* (London: Darton, Longman and Todd, 1994), pp. 158–9.

To enter this struggle, the best first move is to be silent in order to listen. Silence can cause discomfort. Most of our public spaces are filled with muzak; we accompany ourselves with music from MP3 players or mobile phones; hospital waiting areas and post-office queues deliver live feeds of news coverage, adverts or information; homes have the TV or radio on constantly to provide continual background noise. Churches struggle to maintain silence before a service. But even when we do find ourselves somewhere quiet, our mind will happily provide a live stream of thoughts, associations and good ideas to keep us occupied. So how to be silent and listen?

There are several techniques that have developed over hundreds of years. One is to give the mind something to do by repeating a short phrase such as the Jesus Prayer, 'Lord Jesus Christ, Son of the living God, have mercy on me a sinner.' This can be linked with the breathing, earthing it in the body. Some find it easier just to concentrate on noticing the breathing itself without the words. The first move, though, is to close one's eyes. Shutting off stimulation from one sense enhances our ability to use another (I often think of our piano tuner at home who was blind). We do it automatically, sometimes, when we are trying to listen to someone on a bad telephone line or straining to hear a faint sound. We will shut our eyes. Or when listening intently, or speaking of something important or difficult, we take off our glasses and close our eyes, to hear more deeply. And how often, then, we notice the smell of flowers in the room not noticed before – a sign that we have become more still and receptive. Once still and receptive, it is time to start reading.

I say a short prayer before reading – for example, the Psalm verse 'Open my eyes, O Lord, that I may see the wonders of your law' (Psalm 119.18), which expresses our intention to read in order to enter into relationship with God. Or I use a reworking of one of the alternative prayers of thanksgiving at the end of the Communion service:

Open to me the Scriptures, O Christ, and make yourself known

> in the text. Abide with me as I read, that blessed by your royal presence I may learn to walk before you all the days of my life and rest beholding you in the glory of the Eternal Trinity.[65]

It helps Lectio Divina because it makes it plain who we are meeting in the biblical text. Just as Jesus did, on the way to Emmaus, he talks to us and opens the Scriptures to us. We are in his presence when we read, and this has the potential to change us. The final goal of our reading is to rest beholding God in contemplation.

The four elements of Lectio Divina are reading (*lectio*), meditating (*meditatio*), praying (*oratio*) and contemplating (*contemplatio*). Another, more modern description refers to it as the 4 Rs: Reading, Repeating, Responding and Resting. The practice of Lectio Divina encourages us to read the text slowly, several times. Some people advocate reading out aloud as it can help to hear the words as well. What matters is reading with a listening heart and stopping and savouring a word or a phrase if it jumps out at you. When this happens, receive the word or phrase as a gift to be enjoyed in God's presence. When the mind wanders away, gently bring the phrase back into mind and rest in it again. It may well be something that you want to pray with or about. This exercise is, after all, meeting God in or through the text, so entering into conversation with God about whatever has struck you is natural. Simply resting in the presence of God as you are being held by the text is part of it too.

Antony the Hermit wrote colourfully about how we should read when practising Lectio:

> A camel does not need much food. It takes in its food and when it comes home to its stable, it lies down, it brings the food up again

65 The original is 'You have opened to us the Scriptures, O Christ, and you have made yourself known in the breaking of the bread. Abide with us we pray, that blessed by your royal presence we may walk with you all the days of our life, and at its end behold you in the glory of the eternal Trinity, one God for ever and ever. Amen.'

> chewing and ruminating it again and again until the food enters his flesh and bones. In contrast the horse needs much food. It eats much, but it loses very soon what it has taken. So therefore don't be like horses! That means: Don't recite the word of God at all hours without putting it into practice. Behold, take the camel as your model, imitate it! Eat the word of God. Ruminate it again and again, until it incarnates and infiltrates your flesh and bones by reciting each word of Scripture and keeping it there inside you until you have put it into practice.[66]

Ruminating like a camel has the potential to change our lives, enabling us, like Charles de Foucauld, to cry the gospel with our life.

During the long hot summer of 2018, sleep was fitful and disturbed. I remember arriving at the set time for Lectio seriously tempted to give up and have a nap instead. My attempt to stave this off was trying to be present in my body, giving attention to my fingertips, my bottom on my sitting cushion, my knees on the floor. I worked at being absolutely present in the moment, trying to remember that God was there absolutely present to me, longing to speak. I imagine God gets cross with my procrastination about beginning. But instead, when I do finally attend to God, God doesn't say, 'Well, about time too!' but with delight, 'Ah, at last! She has turned up!'

Earlier that morning I had been reading a book about Fr Alec Reid, a priest who ministered in Belfast during the Troubles. He had been instrumental in the peace process, and described how a relationship and reliance on the Holy Spirit was necessary for anyone working as a Christian in a place of conflict. He spoke to my resistance; how difficult it is to attend in silence to God – it can be a real conflict – and how essential is reliance on the Holy Spirit.

---

66 Lucien Regnault (ed.) 'Les Sentences des Pères du Désert', 3° recueil, (Solesmes 1976), pp.148f., where it is part of the 'Vertus de Saint Macaire'.

> … I believe that the Christian will not survive, let alone succeed, at the pit face of the conflict, especially in Northern Ireland, unless he is inspired by the conviction that the Holy Spirit is always with him and is sustained by the confidence in His enabling power which flows from that conviction. This assures him that, whatever the opposition he may have to face, whatever the problems, setbacks, deadlocks, mistakes, disappointments and failures, the Holy Spirit will always be able to counter them, always able to change disadvantage into advantage, threat into opportunity, the negative into the positive just as He changed the Cross of Jesus into the victory of the Resurrection. A relationship of personal trust in the Holy Spirit, developed through constant communication with Him and constant reliance on Him is, therefore, central to the role of the serving Christian in a situation of conflict. [67]

I asked the Holy Spirit to help as I began reading. The passage for the day was Luke 2.15–21 which is the story of the shepherds going into Bethlehem to seek the child in the manger. The text was in Greek (my preference, not only because it is the original language, but also because the Greek is often more vivid and nuanced than English). The first thing that struck me was the word for 'made known'. God 'made known' to them these things; and then, once they have found the child, they 'make known' the words spoken to them about the child. Despite having heard this reading countless times, I had never noticed before that the first to go and tell others about the Saviour in the Gospel were the shepherds. As I sat with the joy of that 'making known' I became aware of the challenge of how do I make Jesus known? How do I make known what has been given to me? Will my life *this* day make known Jesus to those I live with? I resolved to make Jesus known, instead of the frustration, irritation and tiredness that I suspect is what I tend to communicate. Having ruminated as much as I could, chewing

67 Fr Alec Reid C.Ss.R.,'The Role of the Servant of Christ in a Situation of Conflict', quoted in Martin McKeever C.Ss.R., *One Man, One God: The Peace Ministry of Fr Alec Reid C.Ss.R.* (Dundalk: Redemptorist Communications, 2017).

on 'making known', I read and thought of Mary as she 'pondered and treasured all these things in her heart'. This is a verse that is foundational to Lectio Divina, if ever there was one. Finally, I came to the 'before he was conceived in her womb', and found myself praying that I may this day conceive Jesus in my heart and make him known in my life. By this stage I was alert and awake and thankful. Given the struggle to begin to read and pray, I gave thanks to the Holy Spirit.

I noted my three little words – 'make known', 'ponder/treasure' and 'conceive' – and resolved to carry them with me throughout the day, rather like a pebble from the beach in one's pocket, a reminder, sometimes for years, of a place or event. Attending to the word of God daily in this way builds up a collection so that when that text is next encountered, those particular words are still fresh, alongside the new ones that spring up with the current reading. Over time a store of treasures grows.

There is a favourite image of mine which illustrates wonderfully in stone how Jesus was conceived as Mary heard and read the word of God. Behind her is the Scriptures Mary was reading when the angel announced to her that she was to bear a Son. The baby itself is portrayed, speeding down the waterslide from the mouth of God into Mary's ear. We may smile at the medieval tradition of *Conceptio per aurem*, conception through the ear, but the imagination that produced this carving portrays a deeper truth, worth pondering, as we wonder how we too can conceive Jesus and make him known in the world through our reading and crying the gospel with our lives.

Most religious communities have the practice of using the psalms as a major part of their worship, day in, day out. The deep familiarity that results when the psalms are known by heart means a verse will come into your mind, asking for rumination. The words become part of you through the repetition over time, at a different and deep level, which enables attention to the word. Poimen, the Desert Father, describes it like this:

Abba John asked Abba Poimen about the problem that our heart

> is so hard. The old man said 'The nature of water is soft, that of stone is hard; but if a bottle is hung above the stone, allowing the water to fall drop by drop, it wears away the stone. So it is with the word of God; it is soft and our heart is hard, but the man who hears the word of God often, opens his heart to the fear of God.'[68]

The experience of the Psalms, day by day in the Office, is like water dripping on a stone.

The Ignatian way of reading the biblical text is also widely used. The imagination is engaged so we see ourselves there, in the stories and events, alive with our senses to the encounter with Jesus Christ. This way of reading can be particularly helpful if nothing seems to stir when you read. By imagining that you are one of the characters in the story, what would you say to Jesus? What does he reply to you? What do you feel? Jonathan Magonet takes this in a wonderful direction as he imagines how a donkey would read the Bible. Imagining yourself as Mary's donkey on the way to Bethlehem or the flight into Egypt could be a way into an over-familiar text. Such techniques can really help develop attention and engagement with the text so we are open and listening in its company, reflecting and going deeper, allowing the text to lead and challenge what we do and who we are.[69]

We hear the word of God read liturgically. Hearing is our first sense. We don't see until we are born, but a foetus hears from about two months, so our sense of hearing has been developing for seven months before we are born and it is the last sense we lose when dying. This illustrates how important our sense of hearing is. Each time we hear the Gospel read we hear the admonition 'Hear the Gospel of our Lord Jesus Christ according to …' We don't hear 'Read the Gospel of our Lord Jesus Christ'. The act of listening to the word as it is proclaimed offers a significantly different experience. Someone else's

68 *Sayings of the Desert Fathers, The Alphabetical Collection*, trans. Sister Benedicta Ward SLG (London: Mowbray, 1975), Poimen no.183.

69 Jonathan Magonet, *A Rabbi's Bible* (London: SCM Press, 1991).

emphasis when reading can shed different light on the text, just as a different translation or reading in a language that is not your mother tongue can. That difference aids listening. It is a common experience that the hearer will hear something that the reader or preacher hasn't said. When I have asked for a copy of a sermon or looked up a text, and realize that what I heard, what went into my heart, isn't actually there, I know nevertheless it is what I was meant to hear, God's word to me for that day.

Just as the word is heard liturgically, so too is the sermon. How we listen to sermons with our attention focused takes all the preparation needed with the body that Lectio Divina and other techniques, such as the Ignatian way, teach us. We might shut our eyes to cut off distractions and hear better. We might sit attentively, in the faith that God is longing to communicate through the words of the preacher, just as through the words of the Scriptures. Ignoring the distractions of the mind and focusing on the treasure, the 'need of one thing, only' (Luke 10.42) is to be present to the one Person with the whole of your attention as if engaging with a dear friend or someone who was dying. Paying attention to the reaction of one's body to what is said is a crucial part of seeking to hear what God might be saying. Does what is said evoke fear or hope or desire? Where in the body is it experienced? Are you gritting your teeth or sensing a tightening at the back of your throat or in your stomach? Do you feel your lungs expand and your collar bones feel light as if you were going to float up like a helium balloon? Where is the challenge or call of this sermon to you, at this moment? How will it transform you more into the likeness of Christ? What uncomfortable truth is being revealed? Where have you met Christ in its content?

Such questions are of real importance in today's digital age, with clickbaits and other sophisticated marketing, carefully designed to grab our attention. For while information is abundant, our attention is a scarce resource, open to deliberate manipulation.[70] As a result, our ability to pay attention is diminished, and we need consciously to practise paying attention to what we really want and need. Learning to listen to our body or use it to draw us back to what is the most important thing is one way to counteract the subtle devices of the digital media.

When I first came to the convent I was a reluctant reader of the Bible. To be honest, I wasn't much of a reader of anything. But I knew that here in the Bible was the text *par excellence* that I needed to understand. Part of my reluctance was a fear that I wouldn't. My guide at the time counselled making friends with my Bible. When I asked her how I might do that she surprised me by saying that I could make a beautiful cover for it. I did so; and despite my scepticism, found it made a difference. It was one way of saying 'this is a precious book'.

I have brought attention to the art of listening, which is not always the focus when we consider preaching in today's world. I've described the processes used in religious communities, particularly those that are contemplative at heart, of Lectio Divina and Ignatian ways of using the imagination to attend to the text. I've considered how we might let the silence open up the opportunity to hear God speaking to us. Throughout, I've taken it as crucial that we need to attend to our relationship with God and our reliance on the Holy Spirit so that we become a temple of the Word who is Christ. Practising this listening lifelong, attending to God in the silence, transforms us into the image in which we are already made, challenging us to expand our hearts and calling us to incarnate God afresh by crying the gospel with our lives in the world. This practice of listening to the word of God is beautifully summed up in the prayer

> O God, help us to follow the example of Mary, always ready to do your will. At the message of the angel she welcomed your Eternal

70 See James Williams, *Stand out of Our Light* (Cambridge: Cambridge University Press, 2018).

Son and filled with the light of your Spirit she became the Temple of your Word who lives and reigns, now and forever.

Further Reading

Enzo Bianchi, *Praying the Word: An Introduction to Lectio Divina* (Collegeville, MN: Liturgical Press, 1999).

Enzo Bianchi, Foreword by Rowan Williams, *Lectio Divina: From God's Word to Our Lives* (London: SPCK, 2015).

Michael Casey OCSO, *Sacred Reading: The Ancient Art of Lectio Divina* (Barnhardt, MO: Liguori Publications, 1997).

Ghislaine Salvail, *At the Crossroads of the Scriptures: An Introduction to Lectio Divina* (Boston, MA: Pauline Books and Media, 1996).

Martin Smith, *The Word Is Very Near You: A Guide to Praying with Scripture* (Cambridge, MA: Cowley Publications, 1989).

A Sermon for Easter: In Your Resurrection, O Christ, Let Heaven and Earth Rejoice. Alleluia

FRANCES WARD

> In your resurrection, O Christ, let heaven and earth rejoice. Alleluia.

These days and weeks after Easter, have you noticed? We are bathed in a different light.

As I drove south-west through England on Friday, I was filled with delight at the time of the year. The colour: a riotous range of greens, yellows and white. The shimmer of moisture in the air; the soft, intense light. I was reminded again of Gerard Manley Hopkins, the poet who walked and noticed, who wrote of the thrill of a world charged with the grandeur of God; how nature is never spent; of the 'dearest freshness deep down things', and how the Holy Ghost broods with warm breast and bright wings.

This experience of life, abundant life – surging all around us in colour and vibrancy like a Stanley Spencer painting – shows us the resurrection life in which heaven and earth rejoice. The life to which we are born, and in which we continue to live and move and have our being. We find ourselves in the garden in which life began, in which Mary found the risen Christ. The natural world sings the glory of God, now as then, and eternally. It shapes our desires; breaks our heart and re-makes us.

It inspires poets, painters, writers. C. S. Lewis described it like this in *The Voyage of the Dawn Treader.* Caspian and the children are at the end of the world:

> And when the third day dawned ... they saw a wonder ahead. It was as if a wall stood up between them and the sky, a greenish-grey, shimmering, trembling wall ...[71]

This was the frontier between Narnia and Aslan's country, a potent boundary between our desire and the fulfilment of desire.

> Edmund and Eustace would never talk about it afterwards. Lucy could only say, 'It would break your heart.' 'Why?' said I, 'Was it so sad?' 'Sad!! No,' said Lucy.[72]

It would break your heart.

St Augustine, too – he knew this light. He wrote in his *Confessions*:

> There my soul is bathed in light that is not bound by space; when it listens to sound that never dies away; when it breathes fragrance that is not borne away on the wind; when it tastes food that is never consumed by the eating; when it clings to an embrace from which it is not severed by fulfilment of desire. That is what I love when I love my God.[73]

This time of Easter – for, of course, Easter is with us until the coming of the Holy Spirit at Pentecost – this time of Easter is suffused with grace. It is a time of blessedness.

It is a time to think of angels, of the Holy Spirit. Of all life pulsating with God's blessing.

It is a time, as Augustine did, to consider our desires, the

---

71 C. S. Lewis [1952], *The Voyage of the Dawn Treader* (London: HarperCollins (1998 colour edn), p. 251.

72 Lewis, *The Voyage of the Dawn Treader*, p. 101.

73 Augustine, *Confessions*, Bk X, Ch. 6 (Harmondsworth: Penguin, 1961), p. 211.

dearest deep-down desires, and how best to respond.

The encounter between Philip and the Ethiopian eunuch is a strange encounter, full of longing and response, of grace and blessing.

An angel visits Philip. He knows – as perhaps you have done – that angels must be obeyed. He goes immediately to the road between Jerusalem and Gaza, out into the wild country. There he finds a court official of Candace, the queen of the Ethiopians. Imagine him, sitting there, reading in his chariot as the horses are watered. The man, black, beautiful; dressed in resplendent robes. Sonorous as he sounds aloud the words of the prophet:

> Like a lamb that is led to the slaughter,
> and like a sheep that before its shearer is silent,
> so he did not open his mouth.[74]

It would not have been strange for the Ethiopian to read aloud the words of Isaiah. In those days the normal way to read was aloud. The man sits there reading, with his heart aflame with unarticulated longing. Philip asks him if he understands, and conversation begins; a time of teaching about how the prophet Isaiah anticipated Jesus, the suffering saviour. A conversation that addresses the longing desire, and leads to baptism.

The Ethiopian commands the chariot to stop, and both plunge down deep into the cool, green water. Philip declares the words: 'I baptize you, in the name of the Father, and of the Son and of the Holy Spirit'. He is snatched away by the Spirit, and the Ethiopian continues his journey, changed for ever by this encounter, born into the grace of the resurrection life.

Easter reminds those of us who follow Christ that baptism brings us to birth in grace. We live the resurrection life, just as the Ethiopian did. We are there already; the desires of our hearts broken and made whole again and again as we hear the Word, the Logos calling to us, calling us towards the future,

74 Isaiah 53.7b .

in God's love. Towards, as St Augustine says, the everlasting embrace that is not severed by fulfilment, as lesser desire is.

We hear God's call in our lives as the Ethiopian did. So often, like him, we don't understand. All we have is this nagging, yearning for something else, something more to life. We can't put words to it, but it's there, prompting and urging us towards we know not what. Then someone comes, like Philip, spurred by an angel, and helps us to articulate the meaning. Often, then, our life is changed for ever. The word came alive in the Ethiopian. Baptism began the work of grace in him, filling his life with blessing. As it comes alive for us today, our baptism is at work. Just as the world is charged with the grandeur of God, the ordinary becomes extraordinary. The 'dearest freshness deep down things' shines around. We, like the Ethiopian, live our baptism in the new life of the resurrection.

I had a conversation this week with Maddy. She sings in a choir of 20- and 30-year-olds formed out of love of the Anglican Choral Tradition. I was preaching at their church in London and, over supper afterwards, she told me she thought God was calling her. She experienced it as fullness: her life was full in a way she found hard to describe. She looked at blossom on a tree and her heart swelled with thankfulness. She felt the rain on her face, and smiled with the indescribable gentleness. She sang, and breathed in more than air. She loved her job, but thought she had more to give, and that God was calling her to be a priest. For her, it meant following a desire for that fullness of life. A desire that urged her to share the abundance she felt with others. She wanted to give of herself that others might live.

Jesus says, in the Gospel for today:

> If you abide in me, and my words abide in you, ask for whatever you wish, and it will be done for you. My Father is glorified by this, that you bear much fruit and become my disciples.[75]

75 John 15.7–8

To live the resurrected life is to know ourselves surrounded by the grace of God – sight, fragrance, light, embrace. It is to hear the word of the Lord calling us to abide in him as he abides in us. Rooted and grafted into Christ, the true vine, we then bear fruit, fruit that will last.

This passage tells us it is not always easy to follow Christ, and bear Christ's fruit. Our desires will need to be pruned and shaped. We will live through suffering and pain. Did you notice that the passage that the Ethiopian read aloud was Isaiah speaking of Christ's passion? We too will be like sheep led to slaughter. We too will experience humiliation. Share in Christ's death. We will know rejection, and grief. Baptism is through the deep waters of death.

When we abide in the vine, though, that rejection and pain is part of a greater story that gives meaning to suffering. Behind all words and experience we may endure there is God's purpose that is life; the eternal life in which we abide. In which we are fruitful, even in our suffering and pain. The resurrection breaks our heart that we may know the life that is stronger than death.

It may be that you hear that voice, as Maddy has done, as the Ethiopian did so many centuries ago, calling you to greater fruitfulness. A calling, a vocation to abide more deeply in God's love, giving of yourself in service, and in prayer. Perhaps you hear it here, in this wonderful cathedral. Or it may be, like Philip, you are prompted to say to someone else, I see this in you – is God calling you in some way?

We live the resurrection life. There are reminders all around us – from the natural world, in the words we hear, the sounds and sights that speak of God's grace. As the baptized of Jesus Christ, let us live that life in all its abundance, so we abide in God every minute of every day, basking in that glorious light that calls us into greater, deeper, broader love.

For this is the Love that does not let us go. The love that breaks our heart, that we might know the abundant life of God. A love that turns us outwards, to serve others in prayer and action. To live out our baptismal calling to be the witnesses to Easter today, and for eternity.

In your resurrection, O Christ, let heaven and earth rejoice. Alleluia.

6

Attending to the Conversation: The Word of Witness and the Transformation of the World

VICTORIA JOHNSON

What is a sermon for? What is the purpose of preaching? When we think of what preaching is, certain well-worn and often harsh images come to mind. There is the long and boring sermon, the droning on in the pulpit from someone uninterested both in what they are saying and who they are speaking to. There is the exegetical or intellectual sermon that is rather like a lecture, food for the mind but rarely the heart. There are wistful and whimsical 'thoughts' shared with the congregation, like Alan Bennett's excoriating 'Take a Pew' sketch – a parody of the art of preaching that is painful for any preacher to watch, but sadly still as relevant a reflection on today's preaching fare as it was in the 1960s.[76]

We all probably have our own file of sermon types and shadows, some of which never seem to have their ending. When I was a chorister, my sister and I, and the other imps in the choir stalls, would have bets about how long the vicar's sermon would last - 25 minutes was the record. Some sermons can be a test of endurance or seem more like a penance than a celebration of the good news of Jesus Christ.

There are many views about what preaching is and what

76 Alan Bennett, 'Take a Pew', in *Beyond the Fringe* (London: Samuel French, 1961).

preaching isn't. The word 'preach' has so many negative connotations in contemporary culture that it bears some careful unpacking. That word alone evokes the feeling that something is being *done* to someone; we may feel we are being preached at. It also sounds like something didactic and schoolish; we may feel we are being lectured to, with the implication that this is something that needs to be intellectually understood. It has the potential to evoke something of a feeling of condescension, when someone stands figuratively – and sometimes literally – six feet above contradiction. All of these frivolous takes on what preaching is, or isn't, imply that the sermon is a monologue and the listener is passive – simply a repository or sponge for the pearls of wisdom that might or might not be imparted from the pulpit.

A sermon is, in fact, a conversation. In the words of Alan Bennett again, it is facing the 'audience' and speaking to them and with them.[77] In his own world, as a playwright, Bennett is particularly fond of taking the character out of the narrative of the drama in order to draw in the audience through face-to-face conversation. A good sermon always draws people into a conversation, space is made for a response, and there is a hope and expectation that such a response might move from the church into the world beyond.

The word *homilein*, ὁμιλεῖν, from which we get the word 'homily', means to dialogue or converse. It is the word used in Luke's Gospel to describe what the disciples were doing on the road to Emmaus. While they were talking and discussing, Jesus himself came near and walked with them and their lives were changed for ever.[78] A sermon is also about conversion of life, as at its heart – within that conversation or dialogue – there will be a call to be changed or converted and there will be a call to action. A sermon has the potential to be transformative of the lives of those who preach, those who listen and the world into which the community of the faithful is sent.

77 Alan Bennett, Sermon Before the University, 'Fair Play', King's College Chapel, Sunday 1 June 2014.

78 Luke 24.15–17.

In a study conducted by the College of Preachers and the University of Durham, it was revealed that churchgoers actually look forward to the sermon slot. Surprisingly, sermons are generally approached with anticipation by congregations. But strikingly, only 17 per cent of people thought that a sermon had the potential to change the way they live. This suggests that our culture of preaching is not very effective at leaving the confines of church life and witnessing to the world – or, in other words, it is failing to connect.[79]

Many sermons are very good at provoking Christian reflection and contemplation or theological wonderings, but this particular study highlighted that sermons were not so successful in motivating and challenging the listener to look at the world differently or encourage Christian action. Perhaps we are too comfortable in our pews and in our pulpits – and our only desire is to be placated rather than stirred. There is still a shiver of suspicion when a preacher strays into the political arena; there is still the widespread perception that religion and politics don't mix, forgetting that Christ himself was intensely political; he prayed that the world might be conformed to the will of God, which naturally undermined the authorities of the day. There is still a need for a style of preaching that addresses the issues that threaten to undermine the cohesion of society, locally and globally. If the Church cannot speak into the lived experience of the citizens whom it is called to serve and the context in which it is set, it is both impotent and irrelevant and it deserves to be ignored, and so do its preachers.

Fred B. Craddock, the American homiletician, argues that sermons do have the potential to be transformative. They can initiate and sustain movements for social change. Sermons are more than 'words, words, words'.[80] The sermon can be a locus for articulating a Christian response to the demands of the

79 View from the Pew Survey (CODEC, University of Durham and The College of Preachers, 2010).

80 Fred B. Craddock, *As One Without Authority* (Atlanta, GA: Chalice Press, 2001), Chapter 1, 'The Pulpit in the Shadows'.

gospel and a means of recognizing and celebrating the power of the incarnate Word.

When teaching homiletics, I always began by asking the students if they could recall a sermon that changed their life. It was, very deliberately, a big question to try and take us all to the heart of what a sermon is. An even bigger question might be whether any one of us can recall a sermon that changed the world.

A dangerous message

In the last century, one person more than most has demonstrated the power of preaching and the spoken word to shape culture, to challenge the Church, and transform the world for the sake of the gospel of Jesus Christ. Martin Luther King was a preacher whose words influenced world politics, whose Christian rhetoric was used as a tool to speak into the heart of American government. It was impossible to sit passively when he spoke. Here is a man who wrote sermons that literally changed the world and transformed life. His words had power. They were words that stirred a response. They were words that refused to dilute the demands of the gospel.

King's sermon 'Paul's Letter to American Christians' was preached in his home church, Dexter Avenue Baptist Church, Montgomery, Alabama, on 4 November 1956, where he was pastor. This was at first a sermon to his own congregation, and yet it is clearly a foundation for the sermons he would effectively preach to the whole of America and a worldwide audience. This particular sermon was preached many times to different 'congregations'. Between 1956 and 1962, King delivered this sermon 15 times, and these words became a motif in his ministry and a rally-cry to action.

In his 'Letter', King takes on the persona of St Paul, writing an epistle to a community of Christians. Like other Pauline letters, it is written as a conversation, a response to a particular context or need, an observation on what is happening informed by the light of the gospel. King based this sermon on a sermon by Frederick M. Meek, preached at the Old South Church, Boston.

His original copy of that sermon is heavily annotated and deconstructed. King studied the preaching of others as diligently as he prepared for his own. He preached that 'Christ's Kingdom' was a very present reality, one that could not be ignored in a liberal democracy. His words were visionary and prophetic. There is a leanness and efficiency about his language – like poetry, not a word was wasted; like music, his composition was measured and carried cadence and rhythm that could be remembered and imbibed by those who were listening.

King knew what he was doing – he was a student of rhetoric and was certainly no theological slouch. Read his sermons, or listen to them, and marvel at what he does with words. Read his sermons and find evidence of his formal theological education, the influence of Tillich and Barth, and his schooling in Scripture. Read his sermons and find evidence of his interpretation of culture and his challenge to the Church. This is not easy listening. Even when reading this sermon today, even when listening to recordings of it, one is struck by the stark and simple challenge. There is no dissembling or cloaking, or jargon. The challenge, to coin a phrase, is in your face; he is facing the audience. This is a conversation made eye to eye, but a difficult and dangerous conversation where self-centred assumptions and mean prejudices are subverted and, in the light of Christ, quietly ridiculed for the scandal that they are.

His preaching was also an expression of his own faith, his lived theology and of his own Christian witness. In one of his most famous motifs, King cries out that God can transform 'dark yesterdays into bright tomorrows', and can bring 'good out of evil'. This was something that had to be believed first, and then preached. It had to be lived, in order to be transformed into a reality. This was the overarching narrative of his ministry. He believed all things were possible by the grace of God. His words were incendiary because his heart was burning. King could maintain this perspective amid apparent failure, tragedy and setback, because he had complete faith in the transforming power of God. In essence, he practised what he preached and he believed what he said.

Phillips Brooks, the great American preacher, said that preaching is truth mediated through personality, and though I want to say that we should be careful of that, at the same time we are who we are and there is a sense that the words of our sermons, the words of our lips and the meditations of our hearts, are intimately connected to who we are before God. Perhaps it has something to do with whether the listener believes that *we* believe what we say. Preaching is public and brings with it all the trappings of public life and all the challenges of being a public Christian.

However imperfect we each are – with all our flaws and faults and fears – we preach always towards our better self; we are the seed growing towards the light, we are those who are being perfected in Christ. Each sermon becomes an exercise in refining our own faith, our own lived theology; in essence, each sermon is both testifying to Christ and our own personal testimony as one of his followers. Of course, one sermon alone cannot encapsulate everything we would ever want to say, but it is interesting to reflect on what our own preaching corpus says about who we are before God, and how we are growing into the likeness of Christ. The act of preaching makes the preacher vulnerable – we cannot preach in our own strength or by our own worldly authority; we always and only preach as people under God, sustained by the power of Jesus. As the preacher, we are exposed to the divine gaze, to the expectations of the Church and to the critique of the world. We are tried and tested, refined as silver is refined.

When leading pilgrims around the cathedral, I always make a station at the pulpit. I ask one of the group to go up into the pulpit and say how they feel. No one ever says they feel 'powerful' in that position. Everyone says they feel small and insignificant as they draw breath and look down the nave. Standing there, high up and alone, exposes our nakedness before God and before the assembly – there is no glitz, no cover; the preacher stands vulnerable, as one without authority.

We then talk about the calling of every Christian to proclaim the faith that is within them, through the lens of the vocation of those called to preach. We are reminded that we preach in the name of Christ, and whatever vestments we choose to wear when we preach the word of God, we are first to put on the Lord Jesus Christ. Before moving on to the next station, we pray together the words of St Patrick's Breastplate, conscious that on the wall behind any preacher in this pulpit is a sculpture of Christ in Glory, blessing the world, shimmering in burnished gold and bronze, with visible wounds in his hands and his feet. [81]

> Christ be with me, Christ within me,
> Christ behind me, Christ before me,
> Christ beside me, Christ to win me,
> Christ to comfort and restore me.
> Christ beneath me, Christ above me,
> Christ in quiet, Christ in danger,
> Christ in hearts of all who love me,
> Christ in mouth of friend and stranger.[82]

Preaching is an act of witness, and if we extrapolate the meaning of that word to a denouement, the act of preaching makes every preacher a martyr for their faith. For some, like Martin Luther King, this is horribly and violently made manifest. Their words of prophecy, their words of witness, take them to the cross. In the footsteps of Christ himself, they become targets for those who cannot bear the weight or the glare of truth, those who are threatened by the power of a subversive gospel, and those who can only respond to love with venomous hatred. Preaching Christ and

81 Peter Eugene Ball, 'Christ in Glory' (Ely Cathedral, 2000).

82 Words from St Patrick's Breastplate, trans. Cecil Frances Alexander (1818–95).

his kingdom can be a dangerous vocation and it is with fear and trembling that we climb the mountain to preach the word of God to the world Sunday by Sunday.

For preaching a gospel of non-violence, Martin Luther King Jr was murdered on 4 April, 1968. The editors of the magazine *America* asked: 'Will this prophet be heard in death as he was not heard in life? Will the martyr accomplish by his blood what he could not achieve by his words?'[83] It could be argued that Martin Luther King preached not only with his words, but with his whole life. He preached with everything that he was, and everything he was called to be and, in the end, his words from the pulpit were the basis for radical transformation of the world, and a herald of the coming Kingdom. But there is still work to do. His message and his martyrdom give a divided and divisive world pause for thought 50 years on.

Where does preaching take us?

In a book that is now out of print, Canon R. E. C. Browne, formerly vicar of St John Chrysostom's, Manchester, wrote that what a preacher believes about the mode of divine revelation determines the mode of his preaching.[84] Once again, the identity and theology of those who preach shapes the content and message of what they say. This may be an obvious statement, but so often the preacher forgets who they are taking with them into the pulpit – this is not an objective activity. The preacher has an embedded and embodied voice that arises from their context and culture. The God the preacher communicates is a facet of the God they believe in. This is why a long and unfortunate legacy of the preaching tradition is the 'fire and brimstone' preacher who was in effect communicating a God they believed meted out the very same. Jonathan Edwards' sermon 'Sinners in the Hands of an Angry God' is a good example

83 *America: The Jesuit Review.* Some 50 years after the martyrdom of Martin Luther King Jr, equal rights are still threatened.(Editorial, 22 March, 2018).

84 R. E. C. Browne, *The Ministry of the Word* (London: SCM Press, 1958).

of theology and form working together to provoke a fearful response in the listener, but the aim was nevertheless to provoke a response and bring people into a relationship with Christ.[85]

Martin Luther King's theology refused to accept the idea of a holy, righteous Church and a profane and secular world, and instead preached from one integrated theological position. For King, Christ was incarnate. Full stop. King was never going to accept that the Church was an island unto itself. Like St Paul in his letters, his pastoral epistle was directed at American Christians first but as a fractal of a wider message to society as a whole. His preaching refused to be confined to the Church, and this really reflects King's own attitude to religion and politics and perhaps why many of his 'sermons' have been wrongly classified as 'speeches'. He refused to accept the false divisions imposed by both Church and state. In that sense, any sermon is always straddling the convergence of Church and world – making sense of the Church to the world, and making sense of the world to the Church.

What King believed about the mode of divine revelation determined the mode of his preaching. King's non-violent fight for the integration of black and white Americans could also be seen as a fight for the integration of Church and state, or of religion and politics. King was living a theology that promoted the integration of the two spheres in order to make manifest one Christ-centred reality. The Civil Rights movement could be considered as representing a Christological, but non-religious, response to the issue of racism and segregation. This was the situation that King, as figurehead for the movement, was constantly trying to balance and constantly attempting to preach to and beyond.

For King, the gospel was relevant to every issue under the sun and this came through in his preaching and the transformation

85 Jonathan Edwards, 'Sinners in the Hands of an Angry God' (Massachusetts, 1741).

of culture that his preaching was able to achieve. You could say that King, through his preaching, was able to embody a cultural and ecclesial hermeneutic that generated a response, an action, a movement, in the lives of those who heard him. It was in his preaching that he was able to bring Church and world together and present a new vision, a dream, of what might be possible.

Sometimes that encounter was full of tension but it certainly went some way to achieving Rowan Williams' ideal of the Church's call to preach as 'an enterprise which transforms the human world by exposing the deepest human fear and evasions making possible a new kind of existence that passes beyond those fears to a new kind of liberty'.[86] It was a new kind of liberty that King was looking for, and it was heralded in the words of his sermons. Didn't Christ in his 'preaching', by parable and story and challenge, seek to do the same? In his Sermon on the Mount was Christ not articulating the new Kingdom he was physically inaugurating?

Graham Ward in *Cultural Transformation and Religious Practice* suggests that within the life of the Christian Church we have the tools not only to interpret culture, but to transform it.[87] Is it too ambitious to say that preaching could again be a medium for conversion and transformation, not only of individuals but of culture itself? Could the sermon or homily be the place where cultural hermeneutics and ecclesial hermeneutics intersect – the space where each is interpreted or translated to the other, in an encounter that is ultimately transformative for both?

Ward describes cultural hermeneutics as a triad of practical wisdom and learned skill, combined with the habits of everyday living. It could be argued that an ecclesial hermeneutic might also encompass an element of practical, 'people'-centred pastoral wisdom, learned skill and knowledge in the area of theology and the received tradition and the habitus of prayer, vocation and discipleship.

86 Rowan Williams, *On Christian Theology* (Oxford: Wiley-Blackwell, 2000), p. 31.

87 Graham Ward, *Cultural Transformation and Religious Practice* (Cambridge: Cambridge University Press, 2004).

Pope Francis in *Evangelii Gaudium* reflects on the power of preaching to transform. 'Far from dealing with abstract truths or cold syllogisms, it communicates the beauty of the images used by the Lord to encourage the practice of good.'[88]

Preaching is not just a lecture; it is not just about intellectual development. The primary purpose of preaching according to Henri H. Mitchell in his *Celebration and Experience in Preaching* is to provoke and inspire a behavioural response. The ultimate goal, he says, is 'not what the preacher will say about it, but what they [the congregation] will do about it in their everyday lives.'[89]

So preaching becomes a space where Christian virtue can be explored, wrangled with, tested and stretched. It can be a place of becoming for those who preach as well as those who listen, a catalyst for discipleship and a foundation for Christian living; the start of a conversation that we all hope and pray will continue until the words spoken come to life, like the breathing of the spirit into old, dry bones.

Is the sermon, through the preacher, an embodied place of interpretation and a place from which culture can be changed? We have to believe it can be so. Can sermons, can preachers, really change the world as Rowan Williams would hope? We have to believe it can be so. Or, at the very least, can they change the attitude or direction of our worshipping communities so that we turn and look beyond ourselves? Preachers must surely strive for more than 'nice sermon, vicar' as we shake hands at the door? We aim for more than nice. We aim for the Gospel.

Though many say that preaching is outmoded and irrelevant, it is still a medium to be reckoned with and still a medium that is part of the process of transformation that, with God's grace, happens in every act of worship. In a world of 280-character messages and soundbites, the 10- or 20- minute sermon is so alien to culture that it might be considered strangely radical.

There is still power in preaching. Preaching is a speech-act,

88 *Evangelii Gaudium* (2013), p. 142.

89 Henry H. Mitchell, *Celebration and Experience in Preaching* (Nashville, TN: Abingdon Press, 1990), p. 54.

the words that tumble carefully from the pulpit have the power to change lives and transform the world. Perhaps there has been a loss of confidence in the power of preaching; and, rather ironically, in a world of millions where millions of words are written, spoken, texted, we have become a little fearful in the Church about what words can actually do – as if we have lost confidence in the Word made flesh and prefer our words to be disembodied, excarnate, only ever read and never heard.

We anticipate and hope that our preaching leads to something – perhaps a change in attitude, or even affirming some conviction in those who are listening. But perhaps most of all, every preacher dreams that their divinely inspired words might ignite a movement of action in the world beyond the church doors to bring the Kingdom of God that little bit closer.

When thinking of the transformative preacher, Martin Luther King warrants our attention; he was a figure whose preaching forged a movement that progressed from the pulpit into the world, and whose words, stained with his blood, gave us the confidence to dream about what is possible when we proclaim Christ crucified. We can't all be as skilled a preacher as Martin Luther King, but his life and witness can give us confidence in our preaching and its power to transform the world for the sake of the gospel.

A Sermon for Pentecost: The Church is Alive

JOEL LOVE

Aunt Ethel would have been 90 today. They don't make them like that any more, and we miss her. This is a rather sad kind of birthday.

But today is also Auntie May's 90th birthday. She has 2,000 followers on Twitter and has just launched her own YouTube channel. She is active as a volunteer in several local charities and has just completed a sponsored bus ride to Land's End to raise money for one of them. This is a joyful kind of birthday celebration.

There is all the difference in the world between these two aunties, who (until last year) shared a birthday. The difference is that one of them is alive, and the other one is dead.

Pentecost is sometimes called the 'birthday' of the Church. So this morning I would like us to examine whether we think of the Church's birthday as an occasion for nostalgia for a dear-departed relative, or as a celebration of someone who is still vibrant and energetic.

The key indicator of life when it comes to the Church – at least in the Acts of the Apostles – is whether it is communicating, sharing the good news. The real miracle of Pentecost is that each person present heard the disciples speaking about God's deeds of power (Acts 2.11) *in their own language* (see also Acts 2.8).

Any of us who have been alive in more than one decade will have had the experience of learning new words. We need new words for the fashions and technologies among which we live. I still occasionally find myself referring to 'video cassettes' and 'CDs', to the puzzlement of my niece and nephews. And of course our language around able-bodiedness and ethnicity has been utterly transformed for the better over the past 50 years.

A living tradition is one that is constantly being revisited. A living story is one that keeps being re-told. And a living language is one that evolves with use. The Church is alive as long as it keeps interpreting the good news afresh for every generation.

Peter, in his sermon on the day of Pentecost, refers to the prophet Joel and to King David, whose 'tomb is with us to this day' (Acts 2.29). But he does not simply hark back to their day with nostalgia or regret. He links current events to the things they said and experienced: 'this is what was spoken through the prophet Joel'.

Peter is not the first to do this. In Luke's Gospel, Jesus reads from the scroll of the prophet Isaiah, and then says 'Today this scripture has been fulfilled in your hearing' (Luke 4.21). He also says, 'before Abraham was, I am' (John 8.58). So here in Acts 2, Peter is following the example of Jesus.

Based on the number and variety of places and languages listed in Acts 2.9–11, the narrator seems to be making a point about how the good news is capable of being communicated from person to person and across any cultural divide. This is what Jesus wanted his followers to do, when he told them to be his 'witnesses … to the ends of the earth' (Acts 1.8).

The process of communication and interpretation continues throughout the book of Acts: Philip interprets the Scriptures for an Ethiopian visitor (Acts 8); Peter explains the good news to a Roman centurion named Cornelius (Acts 10); and Paul interprets it for some Greeks in Athens (Acts 17). Each of these cultures was different, with its own unique history and forms of expression, just as are the various cultures to which we belong. The process of interpretation is ongoing, and it connects us by an unbroken line to the events of that first Pentecost. It is a sign that the Church is alive.

The minute anyone starts talking about 're-interpreting' a tradition, and especially a tradition in the Church, there will immediately be doubts and reservations raised. How can we be sure we are remaining faithful to the truth that we have received? What happens when our interpretations do not agree? The Church is facing questions like this right now, with regard to gender and sexuality, and also with regard to heaven and hell, sin and salvation, or our relations with other religions. How do we know this is a living tradition, as opposed to a mutation or a virus? The early Church had to face similar questions with regard to the stories and traditions it inherited from Judaism.

The first Pentecost came as a surprise to the disciples, too. They did not make it happen; it happened to them. And it comes as something apparently totally new. They were left to make sense of it by re-examining their understanding of the story they had learned. And their starting point was Jesus. It was Jesus who had told them 'not to leave Jerusalem, but to wait there for the promise of the Father' (Acts 1.4). And so they waited. Interpreting the good news for a new generation or language or context begins when we follow Jesus. And wait.

Pentecost happened when the followers of Jesus were united 'all together in one place' (Acts 2.1). Gathering together physically 'in one place' every Sunday morning is essential training for us as disciples. And the good news is best interpreted when we are 'all together' and 'in one place' spiritually, as well. But the first Pentecost also demonstrated the diversity of God's people. That day, the good news was announced to them by ordinary people, both men and women (see Acts 1.14). This is the point Peter is making when he quotes the prophecy of Joel: 'I will pour out my Spirit upon all flesh, and your sons and your daughters shall prophesy, and your young men shall see visions, and your old men shall dream dreams. Even upon my slaves, both men and women, in those days I will pour out my Spirit; and they shall prophesy' (Acts 2.17–18). So a faithful interpretation of the good news for a new context will acknowledge and celebrate the unity in our diversity. And it will break down the divisions between us.

But, most of all, the first Pentecost happened because the disciples were 'filled' with the Holy Spirit. The Spirit is full of surprises. It takes attention and discernment for us to be surprised by the Spirit. And when we walk and speak in the Spirit we will surprise others too. We may be mocked for this, as the disciples were (Acts 2.15). But people will also be drawn to the mysteries that will result.

And this brings us to the 'fruit' of a good re-telling of the good news. When we find a way to share the good news in the language of the people around us, and are filled with the Holy Spirit, other people will believe the good news and become disciples: 'Those who welcomed (Peter's) message were baptized, and that day about three thousand persons were added. They devoted themselves to the apostles' teaching and fellowship, to the breaking of bread and the prayers' (Acts 2.41–42). As Peter says: 'Then everyone who calls on the name of the Lord shall be saved' (Acts 2.21).

When we celebrate Pentecost each year, it is a reminder that we are part of a living tradition and that we have a job to do. The Church is alive when it is waiting for God, when barriers are broken down and we are united in Christ, when we are filled with the Holy Spirit, and when we interpret the good news to people in a language that speaks to them. The Church has its birthday at Pentecost, but it is very far from being dead yet.

7

Attending to Subaltern Voices: Embodied Preaching as Authentic Christian Discipleship

ANDERSON JEREMIAH

On a hot and humid South Indian summer Sunday morning in 2002, I travelled from my hometown of Vellore to Palligramam, a remote village 60 kilometres away. It was Trinity Sunday in the church calendar and, as I'd just completed my theological studies, I was ready with sophisticated theological insights to share. On that particular Sunday, the congregation of about 20 faithful was anxiously waiting for me to arrive. They had not seen a priest for a couple of months. Without wasting time, I changed into clerical garb and the service began. Midway through the sermon – a complex theological explanation of the meaning of the Trinity within the Christian tradition – there was an uneasy calm and confusion on the faces of the congregation. Following my instinct, I asked them, 'Are you all with me? Do you understand what I am saying?' There was a long pause. No reply for some time, which stirred confusion and discomfort on my part. After more time had elapsed, an elderly person from the congregation hesitatingly raised his voice and said, '*Ayya, saptu rendu nalachu, neenga solrathu onnum puriayala!*' – 'It has been two days since we have had any food, so we cannot understand what you are saying.'

Shocked and surprised, I stopped my preaching and asked them why the Palligramam congregation had nothing to eat.

They explained that as a result of the failure of the monsoon rains, the village lake had dried up and the crops had failed, so they did not have any work. The mango-processing factory in the nearby town that offered daily labour to some of them had to be closed due to the lack of mangoes – also a consequence of the failure of the monsoon rains. With no work and money to buy food, most of the villagers, including the Christian congregation, began using their food reserves, which had eventually run out. I stopped the service, got on my motorcycle, and went to the nearby town to get some food for the famished families. When I returned with some local-made bread, we resumed the Communion service with food. My sermon turned from heavy words on the Trinity to the provision of bread to share.

As a newly ordained assistant curate, my primary task in that pastorate was to visit the congregation of Palligramam, and 17 similar villages, to conduct Communion services and preach on the designated passage, and then go home. This profound encounter with the reality facing rural Dalit[90] Christians stirred me with questions at various levels. What was it to be a priest, especially if he is unaware of the lived reality of parishioners? Had I bothered to know their lived reality, the last thing they needed was a complex theological exposition on the relationship between the Father, Son and the Holy Spirit!

There I was, educated at one of the most prominent Indian theological colleges in the country, which included intensive studies on poor Dalit Christians, standing in the pulpit, preaching theology *at* the people. I assumed I was there to tell them something they didn't know, but the gulf was different to what I had thought. I was the ignorant one – a preacher oblivious to the lived realities of those in the pews. That encounter on that summer day brought me face to face with the lived reality of poor Dalit Christians in India, their sufferings and struggles for

90 Dalit is a term that captures the predicament of a large section of Indian society, who experience untouchability, discrimination and marginalization due to their socio-religious outcaste status.

life. I heard their subaltern voices, reluctant to offend me, and that has occupied my thinking and has become a significant frame of reference for my theological reflections.

I now live in Lancaster, in the north west of England. I find myself wondering whether that Dalit experience in India has anything in common with communities here that experience similar exclusion and marginalization. What experience from those rural parishes in India can help me to explore subaltern perspectives on preaching? How can I now preach in a way that stems from authentic Christian discipleship, grounding the word of God in the lived experience of people?

'Subaltern' perspectives

Indian post-colonial scholars developed the notion of 'subaltern' by drawing on Marxist economic theory, as they engaged critically with the colonial subordination and lower status of South Asian subjects within history and culture.[91] They used the term 'subaltern' to capture the perspective and voice of socially, economically and politically marginalized communities.[92] Subaltern people are dominated to the extent they lack representation and are systematically silenced within an exploitative dominant context. [93] 'Subalternity' can be extended to capture the process and state of being excluded on the basis of race, ethnicity, class, age, gender and sexual orientation. However, it is important not to gloss over the unique existential experiences of disparate communities by using the term 'subaltern', but rather one needs to continue to honour the particularity of such communities, who share a common experience

91 Ranajit Guha, *Subaltern Studies I: Writings on South Asian History and Society* (New Delhi: Oxford University Press, 1982).

92 'Subaltern' is a theoretical category conceived by Antonio Gramsci as part of his political philosophy (*Prison Notebooks*, vol. 1, New York: Columbia University Press, 1992) and later adopted by post-colonial literary theory.

93 Gayatri Spivak, 'Can the Subaltern Speak?', in Cary Nelson and Lawrence Grossberg, *Marxism and the Interpretation of Culture* (Champaign: University of Illinois Press, 1988), pp. 271–313.

of exclusion and marginalization from mainstream society and culture.

The British context has significantly changed in the past couple of decades. The presence of large multi-faith and multicultural communities resulting from increased migration has transformed the landscape of society. Deepening economic inequalities and an increase in poverty has resulted in racial and ethnic conflicts, contributing to a fragmented social scene. To be more specific, my home town, Lancaster, bears the marks of industrial decline and poverty. The city has been undergoing a sort of rejuvenation due to the local university population. However, the large council estates and abject poverty of Lancaster are there for everybody to see. It has been further complicated by significant recent arrivals of refugees and asylum seekers, and the ensuing religious and ethnic diversity. From my experience these communities have become almost cut off from the relative wealth that one can see in other parts of the city. This captures the predicament of many northern towns and cities. So who are the subalterns within this context? In a nutshell, the subaltern are those who are at the bottom of our economic structure, living in poor housing, dependent on the state for their survival, the homeless who are abandoned by the state, the 'unwelcome' migrants, refugees and asylum seekers who are fleeing persecution in their home countries. Women, children and people of colour from a different ethnicity and race also populate this section of our society. The question that begs our attention is, what preaching is meaningful for subaltern people in Britain today?

The mainstream Churches in Britain are yet to fully reflect the racial and ethnic diversity of British society and theologically think with these excluded voices. Crucially, due to the deepening economic disparity, the gulf between the rich and the poor has significantly widened, pushing more people into poverty and making them entirely dependent on food banks for their livelihoods.[94] Churches, too often, are the 'preserve' of the elite, with its declining presence and withdrawal from council estates and poorer communities, which aggravates the lack of connection with the marginalized and excluded communities. The Church of England, in particular, lives with the legacy of colonial economic and political systems that make it hard to respond to the voices from socio-economic subaltern groups, and incorporate them into its theological and spiritual reflections. From a theological and hermeneutical standpoint, subaltern perspective that stems 'from below' would provide a crucial insight in capturing the hitherto silenced, excluded and marginalized voices within the mainstream theologizing and preaching.[95] How might the Church hear the hunger, and respond appropriately?

Hermeneutics of the excluded

Scholars of liberation theology and post-colonial biblical criticism have pursued two prominent hermeneutical processes. The liberation hermeneutical principle commends *seeing*, *judging* and *acting*. This entails bringing a socio-analytical reading of the word of God that begins with the perspective of the oppressed, and explores the possibility of liberation. This has been called 'faith seeking effectiveness'.[96] To read the Scriptures this way is to ask what is the role of the Church alongside the poor and marginalized? Where do we see God's revelation, both in the

94 Joseph Rowntree Foundation Annual Report on Poverty in the United Kingdom, 2018, and Richard G. Wilkinson and Kate Pickett, *The Spirit Level* (London: Allen Lane, 2009).

95 Felix Wilfred, *Asian Dreams and Christian Hope: At the Dawn of the Millennium* (Delhi: ISPCK, 2000), p. 268; also see Marcus E. Green, 'Race, Class and Religion: Gramsci's Conception of Subalternity', in Cosimo Zene (ed.), *The Political Philosophies of Antonio Gramsci and B. R. Ambedkar* (Oxford: Routledge, 2013).

96 Clodovis Boff, 'Methodology of the Theology of Liberation', in J. Sobrino and I. Ellacuría, *Systematic Theology: Perspectives from Liberation Theology* (Maryknoll, NY: Orbis Books, 1993), p. 11; and Jose Miguez Bonino, *Toward a Christian Political Ethics* (Minneapolis, MN: Fortress Press, 1983).

Scriptures and in our current life context? How can preaching God's revelation attend to the lives of the poor and marginalized here and now, and transform word into action?

The answer could be summarized as the 'pragmatic praxis' of Christian faith. This takes us towards an awareness of social and political issues, including culture, religion and ecclesial matters. The key point is that, when reading, interpreting and preaching the word, we should never lose sight of the way people struggle for life.[97] Attending to subaltern voices brings post-colonial perspectives that prioritize the needs of the poor, with an analysis of colonial assumptions and hegemonic intentions that can lead to stigmatization and violation of minority cultures. [98] With this approach, the Bible will be read with awareness of its ideological content, and in the light of post-colonial concerns.[99] Taken together, these two hermeneutical processes enable the development of a contextual subaltern hermeneutics, which can have far-reaching relevance.[100]

Attending to subaltern voices and perspectives calls for a critical self-location, and the recognition that context and interpretation are closely intertwined. It is essential that the particularity of the subaltern person or community is not lost, and so it is crucial that the preacher hears the unique struggles that are faced by the congregation. The global lessons of subalternity should illuminate local experience and not obscure it.

---

97 Fernando F. Segovia, 'Mujerista Theology: Biblical Interpretation and Political Theology', *Feminist Theology* 20 (1)pp. 21–7, (SAGE, 2011).

98 Kowk Pui-Lan, *Postcolonial Imagination and Feminist Theology* (Louisville,KY: Westminster John Knox Press, 2005); and R. S. Sugirtharajah, 'Postcolonial Biblical Interpretation', in R. S. Sugirtharajah (ed.), *Voices from the Margin* (Maryknoll: Orbis, 2006).

99 Philip Chia, 'The Sun Never Sets on "Marx"?: (Marx) Colonizing Postcolonial Theory (Said/Spivak/Bhabha)?', *Journal for the Study of the New Testament*, 30.4 (2008), pp.481–8.

100 Theological praxis is not isolated to liberation theology, but can be traced back in Christian theological history. For more on it, see Elaine Graham, Heather Walton and Frances Ward (eds.) *Theological Reflection: Methods*, 2nd edn (London: SCM Press, 2019).

Preaching and authentic Christian discipleship

Preaching is the means to communicate and interpret the word of God in a particular time and place, to a particular people. It is at the heart of Christian worship. Continuing the long legacy of preaching and prophetic teaching that predates Christ into its Jewish traditions, Christians re-told the story of Jesus of Nazareth to the communities that had not known him. Sermons preached with conviction changed the course of history from the earliest days, with a prophetic voice that spoke into the experience of the subaltern person and community. That tradition of prophetic preaching, with the poor in mind, can be seen through the centuries, for example, with the Wesleyan tradition. Studying the preaching among the Black African American communities, Clardy says that the act of preaching not only offered:

> Critical assessments of slavery and segregation condemned those hateful practices as being contradictory to the Sacred Texts, but also to America's legal and democratic traditions ... crucially, these sermons also sought to speak to the hearts of Black parishioners by offering cooperative words of encouragement that reaffirmed their Christian identity and instilled a sense of pride and dignity.[101]

My early experience in India taught me a crucial lesson about the impact of a sermon within the subaltern context. I found out that sermons need to connect with the lived realities of ordinary Christians, and if the prepared sermon isn't appropriate to help the congregation members in their efforts to lead meaningful Christian lives, then the preacher needs to attend to what will help. The central focus of preaching is to call into focus the Christian faith that the word of God addressed to the disciples, reminding them of their duty to care for their neighbours and the creation so that

101 Brian K. Clardy, 'Deconstructing a Theology of Defiance: Black Preaching and the Politics of Racial Identity', *Journal of Church and State,* 53 (2),(2011),pp. 203–22..

God's love and revelation becomes relevant in every given context. In other words, preaching is an act of Christian discipleship.

Preaching within the context of Christian worship cannot be understood without Christian discipleship. I learned on that Trinity Sunday at Palligramam that my preaching was intimately linked to my lived Christian discipleship. As I've reflected on this, I've gained insight from the Indian cultural and religious tradition of *guru-shishya* relationship.[102] This ancient way understands the *guru* as the source of knowledge, which is passed from *guru* to *shishya* through the spiritual, intellectual and emotional bond between them. The *shishya* leaves behind his social life and devotes his entire attention to the *guru*. The *guru* in turn guides his *shishya* on their path to knowledge and enlightenment. The utter obedience and devotion of the *shishya* is called *bhakti*, which can be understood as a total surrender of ego. For a *shishya* it is his most important duty to spread the values and work of the *guru* to the maximum benefit of humanity, and so become a reflection of the *guru*, spreading the glow and radiance of the *guru* to the wider community. The *shishya*'s perpetual learning shapes his/her activity, and in the process also shapes the community around. Three key dimensions of discipleship are helpful here.

First, a *shishya* (disciple) is primarily defined by his/her relationship to the *guru* (master). In the context of Christian discipleship, Jesus asked his disciples, 'Who do people say that the Son of Man is ?' and they said, 'Some say John the Baptist, but others Elijah, and still others Jeremiah or one of the prophets.' He said to them, 'But who do you say that I am?' Simon Peter answered, 'You are the Messiah, the son of the living God' (Matthew 16.13–16). The knowledge and personal understanding of Jesus born out of an intimate relationship is central to the character of a Christian disciple. Simply put, without the spiritual, intellectual and emotional bond between Christ and us, we will be straying away. The disciple draws from the depth and fullness of God in Jesus through the Holy Spirit, and becomes the conveyance of the abundant life possible

102 This practice is found in many Asian religious traditions.

in Christ. The *shishya* does not merely speak of it, but lives the life of the *guru*. Through an encounter with the *guru*, the Christ, the *shishya* assumes the character of the *guru*. This process entails, in Jesus' words, 'If any want to become my followers, let them deny themselves and take up their cross and follow me' (Matthew 16.24). Denying oneself and taking up the cross is death of the self, death of self-reliance, self-confidence and self-centredness, leaving behind everything and following Christ. Christian discipleship is mapping this experience of unconditional devotion and surrender to Christ on to our human reality.

Second, the *shishya* becomes the extension of the *guru* to the community. Discipleship is not a fenced-off personal devotional path but a practical life that invites others to come and taste Christ in us. Bonhoeffer writes in his *Letters and Papers from Prison* that being a disciple is participation in the being of Jesus, the incarnation, cross and resurrection. He says:

> Our relation to God is not a religious relationship to the most powerful God, this is not authentic transcendence, but our relation to God is a new life in being there for one another, in participation in the being of Christ. The transcendent is not infinite and unattainable tasks, but the neighbour who is within reach in any given situation.[103]

We share the glory and radiance of Christ to the wider community through our life and witness. In the process of surrendering to Christ, we don't lose our identity but are transformed, in such a way that when we are present, Christ becomes present. This is the essence of *guru-shishya* relationship, a sign of a true discipleship, and we all have an invitation to be in such a relationship.

Third, the *shishya* lives out in humility his/her faith and commitment in the community by building each other up in the common life, in spite of their failures. It is evident in several

---

103 Dietrich Bonhoeffer, *Letters and Papers from Prison* (London: SCM Press, 1981), p. 138.

Indian traditions that the *shishyas* were never perfect in their pursuit of a particular *guru*. However, the *gurus* expected their *shishyas* to shape and influence their communities, despite their personal flaws and, if need be, build new ones. To learn from this tradition is to say that Christian discipleship is not just about 'following Jesus' nor particularly about seeking to become 'Christ-like', but is also fundamentally about learning 'on the way', on pilgrimage. The early disciples learned the way of truth as shown by Jesus. There were lingering imperfections and a constant and ongoing struggle with sin. Faithful disciples of Christ will find, according to Jon Sobrino, a Latin-American theologian, ' More happiness in giving than in receiving, give of their own lives, and life itself that others may have life; surrender their lives instead of keeping them for themselves ... they are bearing witness to the greatest love, they are responding in love for their sisters and brothers, to the God who has loved us first; they are living the gift of God'.[104]

The life of a *shishya* is a life lived in tension; there is always a gap between our actual realization of holiness and the goal of God-like holiness to which we are called. Nevertheless, the early disciples made a sincere effort to embody the communal dimension of discipleship. So how can preaching today attend more closely to subaltern persons and communities in the light of this tradition?

Embodied preaching: standing in the breach

Sermons and preaching, as a means of our faith, need to show real sensitivity to those who share the experience of breaking open the word of God; preaching must connect with the lived realities of people. The challenge is to see how the voices of those who are silenced, ignored and marginalized within the Church can be embraced and articulated. Then the Church should engage

104 Jon Sobrino, *Jesus in Latin America* (Eugene,OR: Wipf and Stock Publishers, 1987).

critically with the social and political matrix that determines the context. Within Christian worship, sermons and preaching play a critical role in addressing people's life issues and the context of their lives. A couple of years ago, reflecting on the state of sermons, Justin Welby said about the life of Jesus:

> He does not permit us to accept a society in which the weak are excluded – whether because of race, wealth, gender, ability, or sexuality. Nor did he permit us to turn religion into morality … The old sermons that we have heard so often in England, which I grew up with, which if you boiled them down all they effectively said was: 'Wouldn't the world be a nicer place if we were all a bit nicer?'… That is the kind of moral claptrap that Jesus does not permit us to accept … we are to get involved, we are to get our hands dirty.[105]

To offer authentic Christian discipleship means stepping into the breach between the pulpit and the pew. To attend to subaltern perspectives and voices is to recover the word of God for the people of God, where the text from the Scriptures comes alive and speaks to those who occupy the pews.

Adopting a critical interpretative lens is crucial if a sermon is going to be preached with the conviction of transforming the lives of people affected by the socio-economic realities. There are many ways in which Scripture enables the preacher to speak truth to power, and provoke a change in the situation of the community. This is best achieved by working with the community itself, enabling the Word to be embodied, and in the lived realities of people. Emphasizing the centrality of alternative imagination to preaching, Walter Brueggemann observes:

> Preaching is never a dominant version. Never has been. It has always been a sub version; always a version, a rendering of reality

105 Sermon preached by Justin Welby on 23 January 2015 at Trinity Church Wall Street, New York City.

> that lives under the dominant version … the dominant version of reality among us is violence. If we take that as the dominant version, then the preacher is to subvert by an act of sustained imagination that is an antidote to the culture of violence and this is in the name of God, whose own history is marked on numerous occasions by acts of violence.[106]

Creating space for the text to subvert the situation, to facilitate emancipation of the marginalized and excluded, is central to the subaltern approach. This means Scripture needs to be contextualized and reimagined to inspire the community to a transformative encounter with God.

The fundamental theological task is to question how the revelation of God in Jesus and the salvation of God shapes concrete action in the community. If preaching that attends to subaltern communities is seen as praxis, preaching is not only an act of theological exploration but also instrumental in resistance and emancipation. Contextually aware preaching disrupts the status quo of dominant and exploitative society in order to facilitate liberation. Preaching as praxis may mean that the preacher gets on her bike in the middle of the service, causing a crucial rupture, enabling a faith-seeking effectiveness, not just understanding. Preaching that attends to the subaltern will interpret the word of God and translate the understanding into tangible action to empower the marginalized, or simply to feed them. It will be preaching that is aware of significant social aspects of community life and responds, seeking to expose and challenge the dominant structures that cause the conditions of poverty. Attending to subaltern voices means the pulpit becomes the site of encounter between text and context, God and people, facilitating praxis, and in the process liberating the pulpit and pew. The subjective experience of marginalization of people becomes the context within which the gospel is understood and gains expression in their lives.

---

106 Walter Brueggemann, 'Preaching: A Sub-version', *Theology Today*, Princeton Theological Seminary, Vol. 55 (2), (SAGE, 1998) pp. 195–212.

I learned to preach that day when I realized how easy it was for me to be completely cut off from the lived reality of the people I worshipped with. I learned that day to pay attention to the context of people, and that I had to translate the message of hope into a language that reached into their needs. When Jesus was tempted in the desert he responded to the devil that 'humanity cannot live on bread alone, but on every word that proceeds from the mouth of God' (Matthew 4.4). He was able to refuse the offer of bread, fed already with the rich sustenance of God's Word. The villagers of Palligramam knew they needed to worship God. They didn't need my erudite theological learning, but food that would truly sustain them, in the context of worship.

It is a Christian imperative to hold the people of God at the heart of theological reflection, thought and action. The Indian tradition with which I am familiar encourages me to look to our *guru*/master and heed his invitation to follow him, absolutely surrendering our ego, and embarking on this pilgrimage of learning, so that we may be the living body of Christ in this world, living the gift of God, so that all may have life. In the context of increased fragmentation, mistrust, hatred and bitterness in our faith communities, we are as a Church called, more than ever, to exercise authentic Christian discipleship in building the body of Christ, by being salt and light in the community. Embodied preaching channels the power of God through the body of Christ to become the hope of the hopeless. It empowers the community to re-imagine an alternative society of compassion and generosity. Preaching becomes the very embodiment of hope and new life in the absence of hope and life. Authentic Christian discipleship exemplified by embodied preaching nurtures and enriches the Church in being a living organic community of the faithful, constantly seeking ways to make the gospel relevant and life-giving, chiefly for those who are excluded, silenced and denied life.

A Sermon for Trinity: The Light of the Burning Bush

EDMUND NEWEY

In the eighteenth chapter of John's Gospel, at the fulcrum of the narrative of Jesus' arrest, trial and crucifixion, Pontius Pilate utters a question that the text leaves unanswered. 'What is truth?', says Pilate. His question is a rhetorical one, dismissive, not expecting an answer, because it professes not to recognize the meaning of the terms in which it deals: 'Everyone who belongs to the truth listens to my voice', says Jesus; 'What is truth?' retorts Pilate (John 18.37–38).

The famous irony is that in uttering this dismissive question Pilate is face to face with the truth: Pilate is staring the truth in the face, if he had but eyes to see, ears to hear, and a heart to understand.

At the heart of this sequence of events, in which bucks are serially passed – Annas handing Jesus over to Caiaphas, Caiaphas to Pilate, Pilate to the soldiers.

At the heart of this sequence in which the truth is constantly evaded or simply missed – Peter's denial; the crowd bellowing out their will that a murderer should be set free: 'not this man, but Barabbas', 'nicht diesen, nicht diesen, sondern Barabbam', as Bach's setting in the 'St John Passion' puts it with searing rhythmic force.

At the heart of this serial denial of the truth, all the more tragic because it isn't systematic, but simply the improvised pursuit of the line of least resistance; at the heart of all this stands the man who is the truth.

'Here is the man', says Pilate a few verses later. *Ecce Homo*: here is the man who shows us what a human being looks like when untarnished by the sin that clings so closely to the rest of us: the man who shows us God; the man who is God; the man who, therefore, is the truth:

> Therefore he who shows us God
> helpless hangs upon the tree;
> and the nails and crown of thorns
> tell of what God's love must be.[107]

That is where the story of John's Gospel is going: to the revelation of the glory of God in the shame of the crucifixion. But the portion of John's Gospel that we have heard this morning comes from much earlier in the narrative, from the third chapter. In the encounter between Jesus and Nicodemus the same question that Pilate will ask is implicitly there: 'What is truth?' Yet here the question is posed in a very different setting and mode and it is posed sincerely, not dismissively. Note the differences: first, Nicodemus comes to Jesus, though admittedly under cover of darkness, whereas Jesus is brought bound to Pilate; second, Nicodemus seeks Jesus out, whereas Pilate has little choice but to receive the prisoner brought to him by the High Priest; and third, Nicodemus accords status to Jesus – he calls him 'Rabbi', 'Teacher'; Pilate by contrast puts a question he is not really in a position to understand, 'Are you the King of the Jews?' And though in the end Nicodemus, like Pilate after him, fails to *see* the truth with which he is in conversation, his search for that truth is painstaking and persistent, far from the glib dismissal of Pilate. He too utters a question, but it isn't one that impatiently dismisses the truth, simply one that expresses bafflement, 'How can these things be?'

---

107 W. H. Vanstone's hymn, 'Love's Endeavour, Love's Expense'.

Two questions: Pilate's 'What is truth?' and Nicodemus' 'How can these things be?' Discussing the nature of truth, the fourth-century Church father, Gregory of Nyssa, defines truth as follows:

> In my opinion [he writes] the definition of truth is 'not to be deceived in the perception of what is'. Falsehood is a fantasy present to the mind respecting what is not, giving a specious impression of what exists, but truth is the accurate perception of what really is.[108]

Truth, in other words, is grounded in an accurate perception of being, of the way things are: at root, Pilate's question and Nicodemus' are the same. To ask 'how can these things be?' is to ask 'what is truth?'for 'truth is not to be deceived in the perception of what is'.

But Gregory readily acknowledges that what is simple to define is not simple to find. Most of the time we live our lives either in the condition of Nicodemus or of Pilate: incapable of accommodating our minds and hearts either to truth or to the nature of things as they really are. Yet there are moments – some recorded in the pages of the Bible, some in the lives and writings of the saints, some, however rarely, encountered in our own lived experience – there are moments when the veil that obscures the truth of the way things are is lifted. In theological jargon these are theophanies: revelations of the truth, revelations of things as they are, revelations of God.

Gregory's definition of truth comes in a passage when he is commenting on the most celebrated theophany in the Old Testament, the verses from the book of Exodus that we heard as this morning's first lesson when God reveals himself to Moses in the bush that burns but is not consumed. In particular, Gregory is reflecting on God's first words to his servant: 'Come

108 Life of Moses, II:22.

no closer! Remove the sandals from your feet, for the place on which you are standing is holy ground' (Exodus 3.5). 'By [the light of the burning bush]', Gregory writes,

> we are taught what to do in order to stand within the rays of the true light, namely that one cannot run with bound feet up to that height where the true light has appeared without removing the dead and earthly covering of skins from our soul's feet, the skins which originally became fastened to our nature when, by disobeying the divine will, we were stripped bare.[109]

This is a wonderful instance of allegorical interpretation: the ancient tradition, Jewish in origin, of reading the Bible at a more than literal level, allowing its truth to seep into every aspect of our being. Gregory does not deny that Moses did indeed literally remove his shoes at the sight of the burning bush and the sound of the divine voice. But Gregory wants us to understand that a simple physical action – unbinding the skins that served as shoes to protect the feet from the heat and stones of the desert – can resonate at every level of our being. He takes us back to the Garden of Eden, to the story there of the origins of clothing in the sense of shame that came with Adam and Eve's first disobedience. As I tie my shoelaces each morning I don't generally think that in doing so I am acknowledging my status as a sinful son of Adam, but when I take my shoes off and run barefoot in the garden with my children I do sense something sacramental:

> Generations have trod, have trod, have trod;
> And all is seared with trade; bleared, smeared with toil;
> And wears man's smudge and shares man's smell: the soil
> Is bare now, nor can foot feel, being shod.[110]

When you remove your shoes, you become reacquainted with an

109 Life of Moses, II:22.

110 Gerard Manley Hopkins, 'God's Grandeur'.

underdeveloped sensory faculty. To do so is at once an intensely personal experience and one that situates us, as Gregory sees, in a line continuous with our ancestors in those original scarcely imaginable times before sin was an inevitable component of what it is to be human.

God who reveals himself to Moses in the burning bush names himself as *Ehyeh asher ehyeh*, rendered in most translations as 'I AM WHO I AM'. But the utterly stable reality implied in that translation is misleading. Ben Quash has offered this as an alternative: 'I will happen as I will happen'; or even 'I will come to be as I will come to be' (*Found Theology: History, Imagination and the Holy Spirit* (London: Bloomsbury, 2013), p. 49). This state of inexhaustible coming to be is what is revealed in the bush, burning but not consumed, and it is the state promised in the eternal life that Jesus promises at the conclusion of his encounter with Nicodemus: 'For God so loved the world that he gave his only Son, so that everyone who believes in him may not perish but may have eternal life' (John 3.16).

Perhaps on Trinity Sunday you were hoping for a sermon expounding the mysteries of the triune God. I haven't offered that. What I have tried to offer is a sermon that at least points to the times and places where the triune God may be found. The doctrine of the Trinity, like all orthodox teaching, is a carefully formulated piece of grammar offering a series of 'protocols against idolatry'. Far from being a straitjacket, orthodox doctrine is liberating. It invites us to explore the length and breadth and height and depth of truth; of the nature of things; of humanity; of God. To look expectantly for the God who ceaselessly wills to reveal Godself to us, happening as God will happen, that we may become what we were created to become: free beings, freely loving the God who loves us so much. 'Remove the sandals from your feet, for the place on which you are standing is holy ground.'

8

Attending to the Joy and Terror of Preaching the Embodied Word

RACHEL MANN

It is Saturday 8 July 2017 and London is buzzing. By the time my train arrives from Manchester, festivities have spilled down into the Underground. Young and old carry rainbow flags, and pink, blue and white ones too; many have multi-coloured face-paint on their cheeks and there is energy and joy. Some, when they spot my black shirt and dog collar, glare at me; others smile indulgently. I smile back. It is a day of feasting, after all. It is hard not to be caught up in the celebratory atmosphere.

When I arrive at my final Tube stop and step out into the street, the heat and noise is stifling – if noise can be stifling. I'm used to London. It can be exhilarating. These crowds, however, are overwhelming, despite the mood of joy, fun and delight. There are tens of thousands gathered near Piccadilly Circus and along the West End. I do my best to slide and manoeuvre through the hundreds, the thousands, of partying people. By the time I arrive at church to preach, I am exhausted, a flesh-bag of sweat.

It is Saturday 8 July 2017 and I've been invited to preach at the Christians at Pride Service at St James, Piccadilly. Although I've spoken at Pride events around the UK before, this invitation feels especially significant. London Pride, despite the size and importance of Brighton and Manchester events, still feels like the motherlode. Preaching at this event feels weighty and pregnant with significance. For, if Pride has, for good or ill, become something of a corporate jolly in recent years, the Church continues to be a site of trauma for LGBT* people. The fact that on the day of the Pride parade, hundreds of Christian LGBT* people and their allies are to gather in a West End church feels important and necessary, not least because of the wider Church's ongoing equivocation about the status of queer people. The Pride service, I sense, shall be an articulation of uncomfortable, but still necessary truths: of pain, yes (there is to be testimony from a person who'd survived 'conversion therapy'), but also hope and solidarity.

In this chapter I want to explore the work, theological and otherwise, that can be accomplished when one preaches at a service like that of Christians at Pride. I want to suggest that rather than being esoteric or marginal or – in their status as 'one-offs' – of lesser value than sermons in the 'ordinary' weft of church life, the occasional sermon foregrounds what all sermons can accomplish. I want to suggest that such 'sermons seldom heard' – to use a striking phrase of theologian Annie Lally Milhaven – speak beyond their particularity, specificity and rarity, in part because of their particularity.[111] They reveal the structural possibilities held in the genre of preaching; its joy and terror. I shall suggest that if the sermon I preached at Pride 2017 acts almost as the acme of an occasional sermon, it powerfully indicates that making sermons, the act and art of preaching, is the inspired work of particular bodies and, therefore, of located grace. Indeed, that it is an embodied matter, which not only embodies words but finds its life in the work of Jesus Christ – the living, embodied Word.

111 Annie Lally Millhaven (ed.), *Sermons Seldom Heard: Women Proclaim Their Lives* (New York: Crossroad, 1991).

The facts of a preachment

I want to explore some of what might be called the 'wider' facts of preaching through my specific experience of preaching at the Pride service. To do that, it will be helpful to offer a 'thick' – that is, detailed and layered – account of how I found preaching at the Pride service. Listed below are some of the factors which, as I've attempted to recapitulate the events of the service, have struck me as significant for reflections. Necessarily, they reflect my view of affairs, recalled at leisure, from a distance. They are partial, limited and partisan, though, I trust, no less interesting for that.

First, space matters. I had been inside Wren's seventeenth-century church before, but not to preach. When I arrived I was struck by its scale. It is not a vast church, but it has presence. There are pews and a gallery, shaped around a very wide and open chancel. The walls – white with gold embossing – and the elegant pillars contrast with the dark wood of the pews and gallery. It has a kind of calm rationality that lends it to thoughtfulness rather than emotion. The building speaks of stability and (regal) power and proportion, values significant in the era of the Restoration when it was built, as the nation healed after upheavals of Civil War and the Commonwealth. It is a building that models confidence, financial and otherwise.

As I and other ministers prepared for the service, I seem to recall being encouraged to preach from the chancel area, from a small dais, rather than a pulpit. I could see grounds for this. This was going to be a relatively informal service, drawing together people from a wide variety of Christian traditions. However, I was nonetheless alert to the context of this building; its structural power (tied, albeit unconsciously, to a Church's instinct to model 'power-over') was a dynamic I would have to negotiate in my preaching. The instinct of the organizers was that I should negotiate this dynamic by not using the pulpit.[112]

The planning team had given considerable thought to the

112 The internal one! Unusually, St James has an external pulpit too.

biblical texts to be used in the service, especially given the fact that some biblical texts have been used as 'texts of terror' against LGBT* people. There had been a fair amount of toing-and-froing between me, as preacher, and the liturgical planning team. Generally, my instinct is to try to stick with the lectionary; ultimately, however, we agreed to run with texts that have been read as modelling grace, hospitality and welcome. For example, the Old Testament reading was the section of Genesis in which Abraham encounters the visitors at Mamre. I decided to preach on the Gospel reading, Luke 24.13–32, the Road to Emmaus reading. It is one of the richest, most potent texts in the Bible; it is one I have returned to with delight and anticipation. Its themes – of seeing and unseeing, of Christ 'coming out'/of revealing himself or of being seen for who he is, as well as the sense that the disciples walk away from a site of trauma, rumour and bewilderment only to find hope and hospitality – struck me as rich ones for the service.

The service was delayed. It was due to start at 4 p.m., I think, but we had to delay because many of those walking in the parade were delayed. This delay, combined with the heat and my being on the edge of dehydration left me feeling physically discomforted. I was sweltering in my choir dress and simply wanted to get on with the service. I was in danger of becoming tetchy or losing my focus. As someone with a hidden disability, sensitive to high temperature (I have no colon and therefore no simple way of recycling water within my body), being dehydrated is a serious risk. Also, I was nervous. I'm an experienced preacher. I've preached at some grand occasions and in grand places. Nonetheless, I felt anxiety. This was the kind of preachment that had to negotiate a community's pain, fear, hope and so on. The delay did nothing to allay my fears that I wasn't up to the job.

At the same time, as we stood at the back of the church, it was lovely to see so many of the parade walkers, smiling, hot and exhilarated, stream into the service. It was wonderful to recognize many and exchange a few words. However, it only added to the sense of unreality. There I was, along with the other clergy and lay ministers, dressed up to the nines for divine worship, and in flowed a rainbow collection of people, giddy from celebration. It was a meeting point of glitter, unicorns and cassocks. The ministers – not exactly dressed modestly – were dressed as one might be for Evensong in College Chapel, while most of the congregation were dressed for partying down Old Compton Street. Finally, 25 minutes late, the procession set off.

As I hope this description has already made clear (even if it is a seemingly banal point), sermons are located things. They take place as part of wider liturgical gesture. My sermon was part of a service that was a curious combination of formality and informality; most of the clerical cast were Anglican and dressed as one might expect traditional Anglican priests to dress for a non-Eucharistic service; the liturgy combined elements of Iona, Anglican and *ex tempore* work. The music included classic evangelical/charismatic songs alongside familiar hymns and there was space for testimony and storytelling. It was deliberately non-Eucharistic.

It was more than strange to preach into that context, especially when set alongside my anxieties about my personal adequacy for the task set before me. I am, perhaps, a little more comfortable with formality than the preaching context offered, though my background in an evangelical-charismatic church and my instinctive sense of theatre meant I wasn't overly intimidated, irritated or ill at ease. Certainly, when it comes to occasional sermons in large venues I've tended towards the formal: ensuring that my words are written down, preaching from a pulpit, and so on. Perhaps that has reflected the nature of those occasional preachments – they've often been in cathedrals, college chapels or on festal occasions. Yet, at the same time, St James Piccadilly is no tin hut. Far from it. Its grade 1 architecture lends itself to drama and theatre; it is a kind of preaching barn. It is a place – with its white and gold walls and rational proportions – that says, 'The Word is the Thing.'

I had prepared carefully for this sermon. Given what I've already said, that should not surprise you. This preachment was a big deal for me. What may surprise you is that when I stood up to preach, all I had was a 'post-it' note with a couple of phrases scribbled on it. I looked at it as I stood. It said something like 'site of trauma … site of hope' and, as I prepared to walk to the centre of the chancel to pray, I dropped it on my chair. I slid off my sandals and walked into the heart of the church, prayed, and spoke.

I spoke of hope and the surprise of grace, and I spoke of trauma and exclusion. I spoke of how the Church has changed and how it has not changed, for both good and ill. I sought to speak of Jesus Christ. I spoke of the LGBT* community being like Cleopas and the unnamed disciple walking away from a site of trauma and encountering hope – an intervention of Love – on the road, of how the LGBT* community might discover the texture of Love's fullness in the communion of broken bread; having made my case, I spoke also against this idea. I suggested that the story might equally tell of the Church walking away from the site of a trauma of its own making – its rejection of LGBT* people – and discovering a queer Christ offering it reconciliation. I spoke of how, sometimes, LGBT* people walk away from the Church as a site of trauma, and when Christ meets them on the road and offers bread and hope, they do not stop in Emmaus, but walk on and keep on walking, leaving Jesus behind. And they do so understandably.

I've described my anxiety and inadequacy. At a deep level, I wonder if I might also speak of 'terror'? That's risky. It would be to suggest that – in old-fashioned language – I encountered something of the Sublime in preaching into that context, something more than the 'heart-pounding' that comes from a little adrenaline coursing round one's body. And yet … in preaching in a building that models something of the Beautiful (proportionate, ordered and measured), I encountered something. Perhaps I was more dehydrated than I realized. Would it be wrong to say that, despite the large congregation and the significance of the building, my experience of preaching that day was as if all 300 plus of us were in an intimate space? Yes, I projected, I performed, I deployed all sorts of rhetorical tricks and tropes, but in the midst of theatre it was as if we stepped outside of the ordered space (and time) into one that was more startling. It was as if we were eyeball-to-eyeball and we were not afraid. Generally, one has no desire to be so intimate with anyone unless it is with one's lover. Yet, I sensed it was where I was called to be; I sensed others were there with me. There was, in the intense dynamic of preaching, strangeness and intimacy. There was embodied grace. It is to what I mean by this that I want to now turn.

What also happened?

A sermon might appear to be many things. If one were to pick up a collection of sermons – perhaps the sort of erudite collections considered suitable for the instruction of well-heeled, white 'ladies' in a Jane Austen novel – one might suggest that a sermon comprises acres of words on a page, sealed safely inside (calf) skin. It is – on this kind of picture – an anachronistic object of power and cultural formation. A collection of sermons might be read as a gathering-up of words of power and authority, perhaps rendered safe and suitable for the genteel to consume privately; indeed, one might claim that those classic, leather-bound, eighteenth- and nineteenth-century collections of sermons act as metonyms for authorized, white, middle-class, clerical power.

Equally, one might read the notion of sermon and preaching through the language of art. When we, at Manchester Cathedral, established the Manchester Sermon as a secular literary series in 2010–11, the invitation letter I composed contained this: 'Many of the language's greatest poets and thinkers, from Donne through to Newman, have used the sermon as a place for pushing the boundaries of English and reflecting upon what it means to be human. Dr Johnson famously noted, "that sermons make a very considerable branch of English literature." We are seeking to rescue the sermon from its current unappetizing state and re-establish it as an interesting and vibrant literary form.' To tempt noted writers like Jeanette Winterson, Sir Andrew Motion and Elif Shafak to come and 'preach', we pitched the concept as centring around carefully crafting and making of words; as a work of writing, of literature, suitable for the finest literary writers.

If a sermon is made to be preached, however, it is never mere words, no matter how carefully crafted or of literary significance; it consists of words made and delivered by particular/specific bodies into particular times and places; sermons are delivered/spoken into particular times and spaces, surrounded by other words, gestures and witnesses in dynamic relationship with the sermon. In that sense, to print a collection of sermons is never hugely interesting, unless one treats the collection as a mutually informative, dialectically dynamic context in which sermons speak into and read each other;[113] as a context in which the words then interact with the reader or interlocutor. To preach, however, is embodied performative discourse, undertaken by particular bodies in a wider assembly of bodies, the body of Christ (the Church, the liturgical, or Eucharistic assembly, and so on).[114]

What I want to draw out, however, is the embodied performance as theologically suggestive and instructive; how it acts as a gesture

113 One might contra-argue that to collect sermons in such a manner is a deeply subversive act, especially if they're intended for a genteel, 'feminine' audience: rather than being a means of instructing minds in passivity and gentleness, the sermon might give people ideas! Of course, such is one of the issues of placing holy texts like the Bible, the Tanakh, or the Koran in people's hands – they might read them and find the material to critique authority/authorized readings.

114 While it falls outside the scope of my exploration of preaching at a Pride service, it's worth noting (as an example), in Eucharistic contexts, 'the sermon' sits within the Ministry of the Word, breaking open the Word and gesturing towards (the Ministry of) the Sacrament in the world. The preacher crafts words in the Word; her body is offered for the animation of the body and is animated by that body.

towards what I've labelled 'embodied grace'. I shall attempt to explore this via a discussion of the bodily, initially, a discussion of feet.

One of the things an attentive reader may have noted in my earlier account of preaching at Pride is the line, 'I slid off my sandals, walked over to the centre of the chancel, prayed, and spoke.' Those who imagine they know me well will perhaps be inclined to say, 'Typical Rachel, she has to be different; she loves her moments of theatre.' There is truth in this. I do rather enjoy a little theatre, as I indicated in the previous section. I am alert to the possibilities of the body: the way in which it may communicate. These include, in a preaching context, the words one uses, the rhetorical techniques, whether one chooses to use a script or notes or – as I did – go without. I am alert to the way in which the *vested* or *clothed* body communicates, just as I'm fascinated with the inscribed/tattooed body. I am alert to the dynamic between bodies and the spaces into which they speak, and the way space and context speak and sing back. So, yes, my decision to preach discalced, might be read as 'theatrical', but it was much more than that. Not least, given how hot I felt it was a practical consideration! Yet, there was still more. Sometimes, when we stand to speak, only the body can speak for us.

The discalced gesture was a theological-semantic gesture. In a recent article, Bonnie Miller-McLemore, when reflecting on the nature of the body, speaks of 'literal physicality'.[115] She draws out the particularity of bodies. Susannah Snyder, thinking about the importance of this physicality in relation to migration and refugees, notes, 'every person's footprint, gait and even dynamic plantar pressure patterns are unique: they carry and tell a distinctive human story'.[116] She adds, 'faces, notably Brown and Black ones partially covered by beard or veil, are all too easily stereotyped particularly by those of us who are

115 Bonnie Miller-McLemore, 'Embodied Knowing, Embodied Theology: What Happened to the Body?', *Pastoral Psychology*, 62 (2013), pp. 743–58, 744.

116 She draws on the work of Todd Pataky, 'Gait Recognition: Highly Unique Dynamic Plantar Pressure Patterns Among 104 Individuals', *Journal of the Royal Society Interface*, 9 (69),(2012).

White. Feet also bring us somehow onto holy ground: it is on his two soles, heels and toes that Moses stands before the divine theophany in the burning bush (Exodus 3.5).'[117]

The significance of discalced feet in the Tradition is further indicated in the importance of the practice among Religious, not only as a signal of vows of poverty, but also of obedience to and trust in God. Feet, of course, also seem to mainline into our anxieties and fears about the body. They almost act as an icon of that which many of us/our culture abjects about bodies: witness how bizarrely people behave around ritual foot-washing on Maundy Thursday. I've witnessed Cathedral Precentors panicked about finding enough 'volunteers' to take part in the ritual. Those who volunteer usually wash their feet before they're washed. Feet represent something deep about our relationship with our bodies: feet bear the weight of (most) bodies; they carry us and leave marks as distinctive as fingerprints; they can be the means, when brought into consort with powerful legs, of kicking in doors; they are read as unlovely, dirty, necessary and valuable.

In some ways, my decision to slip off my sandals was instinctive. Yes, I was hot; yes, I am theatrical, but there was something else. It had to do with the location, and the congregation/gathered community. It had to do with the liturgical context, and the interactions between them all. Thinking back now, I remember looking across towards the heart of the chancel, just before I stood to speak, and being alert to how neat and proper the space felt. All that stone/marble on the floor; the neat rows of pews and balcony; the vision of stability and solidity gestured towards by the architecture and church furniture. By contrast, I considered the gathered community – colourful, queer and strange, a large and curious mix of celebration, anticipation and anxiety, even anger reflected in their faces – bringing animation and oddness

117 Susannah Snyder, 'Washing Walking and Wounded Feet – Pedetic Textures of a Theo-Ethical Response to Migration' (Keynote Address: The Society for the Study of Christian Ethics, 19 October 2018).

into a curiously static and traditional space and context. And there I was, sat there, dressed pretty much as all clerics in the Church of England have dressed for non-Eucharistic services for centuries. Conscious that I was both simultaneously a priest in the Church of England, as well as a queer woman. For some reason, to preach discalced became a way I might embody that complexity; that 'interstitial' reality. By taking off my sandals, I allowed my queer body, via unshod feet, to be exposed to the cool, timeless marble of the building. I stood and felt the cool of the stone flow up through my body. I felt earthed, and engaged in something that – quietly, discreetly – queered the praxis of preaching.

This might all sound quite absurd, or hippy-dippy. It might seem far too specific to have anything to say into the wider praxis or liturgical work of preaching and sermon-making. I've spent most of this chapter talking about how a particular, fragile and precarious body dynamically participates as a preacher in a wider liturgical drama. In the closing section, I want to reflect on how this particularity may speak into wider preaching praxis.

The utopians, the tragedians, and the rest of us …

Late in her career, the philosopher Gillian Rose gave considerable attention to the ways in which the polarizing and, as she saw it, limiting binaries of postmodern discourse might be resisted. Working primarily in the areas of politics, jurisprudence and the law, she developed concepts like the 'Third City' and the 'Broken Middle' to indicate the aporia and possibilities of embodied, lived subjectivity.[118] The Broken Middle represents the complex,

118 Gillian Rose, *The Broken Middle: Out of Our Ancient Society* (Oxford: Wiley-Blackwell, 1992). For an analysis of the concept of the Broken Middle, see Rachel Mann, 'Presiding from the Broken Middle', in *Presiding Like a Woman: Feminist Gesture for Christian Assembly*, ed. by Nicola Slee and Stephen Burns (London: SPCK, 2010), pp. 133–9.

lived ground or space between binaried philosophical or judicial or theoretical concepts. Rose posits it as a third term between, for example, the universal and the singular, the law and ethics, and actuality and potentiality. In Kate Schick's summary, the Broken Middle is a critique of 'the old, for its prescription and progressivism, and the new, for its rejection of the struggle to know and to judge'.[119] She adds, 'the difficult … work of the middle … sits between tragedy and utopia: acknowledging the profound brokenness of actuality, while refusing to be paralysed by this brokenness'.[120] It is indicative of both a place of liminality, interstitiality, and the 'in-between', one that may be negotiated with hope, trembling, and possibility by particular lives/bodies.

My account of preaching at Pride – something that many might argue falls too readily into the singular, atypical, and unusual – represents, I suggest, one kind of resistance to the polarizing temptations of the utopian or the tragic. For, that sermon reveals how, in a liturgical drama,[121] the work of preaching is embodied, limited and contingent. It carries the traces of sex, gender, ethnicity, class; it carries the traces of a particular set of footprints. Sermons are the works of particular bodies in community and in tradition. Yet, they are not – if they are serious wrestlings with the word – mere singularity. Arguably, as they attempt to speak of the Word with words, they represent a point of mediation between the contingent and the eternal; between a kind of (platonically conceived) Word, that utopian vision of Ur-language, and the tragedy of words

---

119 See Kate Schick, *Gillian Rose: A Good Enough Justice* (Edinburgh: Edinburgh University Press, 2012), pp. 36–7, as well as section 1, part 2. Gillian Rose's *Mourning Becomes the Law: Philosophy and Representation* (Cambridge: Cambridge University Press, 1996) represents her attempt to revisit the concept of the Broken Middle through the political metaphor of the City. In our European discourse, the politics of reason ('Athens') vies in tension with the politics of the idealized ethic ('New Jerusalem'); behind and between them lies the Third City, the politics through which we live. See, especially, Rose, *Mourning*, pp. 20–35.

120 Schick, *Gillian Rose*, p. 37.

121 And, when we preach in the midst of the Eucharist, into *the* liturgical drama of the Christian faith.

that never quite find sufficient grip on the world, and become lost in meaning. My sermon at Pride was deeply embedded in its context, but – as with all serious sermons – surely a deep wrestling with the limits of what the Word permits and commends.

Just as Jesus Christ becomes embodied Word – incarnated as a particular body, in time and space – whose incarnation speaks the very grace of God, so might preaching be seen as a species of his work now: a kind of embodied work that models the possibility of grace as it gestures towards God's Kingdom. For, surely Christian formation is about negotiating the dynamic that insists, on the one hand, we live on the promise of a Kingdom that is abundance, always more-than-enough, gift and grace, yet is ever shadowed by tragedy, our lived limitations and the bitter facts of our incapacity to save ourselves. To preach is to speak into the gaps between abundance and limitation. The preacher's work can only appropriately be done by bodies, limited and precarious and barely up to the task; she offers words that always risk failure, that are barely adequate to sing grace. Her work, metaphorically and sometimes literally, is a work of risk: daring to walk on holy ground with feet – grubby, unique, capable of carrying us up high mountains or making marks on the moon, but also readily abjected – we fear are insufficient to the calling. The preacher's work is done in the knowledge that she might be destroyed in the presence of the Holy.

Ezra Pound suggests that poetry is 'the news that always remains news'. In so far as liturgy has a family resemblance to poetry, my sense is that the formal newness of the liturgy – of which I want to say 'the sermon' is part – lies in the dynamic between the formal, the authorized and the embodied particularity of liturgical gesture. The sermon – ever in the hands of particular bodies – represents, in the moment of the Word, the intervention of tricksy, wondrous and dangerous words. To stand in that space and dare to speak is potentially to speak into a space of both terror and joy.

If my experience of preaching at Pride represents, for me,

the acme of an intense, risky preaching moment, might it not simply be a gathering up of what we might hope to find in all the opportunities we might have to preach? Those of us who preach regularly and, arguably, excessively, can find the praxis becomes 'domesticated', 'everyday' and 'ordinary'. But, as I've attempted to suggest, at a theo-symbolic level, to preach is to place oneself in an alarming place – a place where one might encounter joy rather than pleasure, terror rather than fear. It is to risk intimacy. It is to allow our feet to touch holy ground. It is to come face-to-face with our own inadequacy while risking being torn apart by the Word. It is grace, and we are never prepared for it.

A Sermon for All Saints: Ordinary Saints

ANDERSON JEREMIAH

One day in my Early Christianity lectures, I asked my students to define who is a 'saint' and then to name a few. Someone said, 'A saint is someone who is either deified, dead, or different.' Indeed the moment we hear the word 'saint', it conjures up several images in our minds. Stained glass windows, images of men, mostly white men with halos. Most of my student's example fell into two categories.

First, there were those saints who are practically deified. Ancient stories describe them to be godlike and we tend to envision them with halos. They are the superstars of past ecclesiastical piety. You can easily tell who they are because 'saint' is in their name – that is, St John, St Mark, St Augustine and St Francis. All are apparently removed from us by a large gulf of time and seemingly unmatchable holiness.

Second, there were people in the past who died in the faith, and in most cases died for the faith due to intense persecution. Saints are individuals who were willing to go against the flow of the ordinary, put their bodies on the line for their faith and were killed. This list included St Stephen and St Peter and more modern names, like Dietrich Bonhoeffer, St Theresa and the newly sainted St Oscar Romero. These people were lifted up in our memory, in most cases, because some of their actions were

Christ-like. But if we look closely, we quickly discover that they are just like us.

Saints, I believe, share our common ground and open a place in the circle of forgiven sinners. 'Forgiven sinners' is the standard New Testament designation for saints. They don't necessarily work for the stained-glass-window status. If you read early life stories of some of the saints, many are pretty dodgy! But the difference is, as William Stringfellow, an American lay theologian put it, saints are 'those men and women who relish the event of life as a gift and who realize that the only way to honor such a gift is to give it away'.[122] The implication of this understanding is that we, who are imperfect and deeply flawed human beings, can be called by God through Jesus Christ, crucified and risen for the world, as saints in the making – past, present and ongoing. Martin Luther describes saints as 'sanctified sinners'.

In today's Gospel (Matthew 5.1–12), Jesus addresses his followers-who-would-be-saints. It is not a template for how society works. It is the pattern of life where saints are in the making. The details of Matthew's setting are significant. Jesus had been travelling, preaching and healing people throughout Galilee and Judea. There was a great crowd of disciples and a greater crowd of sick and troubled people waiting for him. Picture desperate people jostling, pushing, begging, clamouring, demanding, all reaching for his healing touch. It is a sight more alarming than inspiring. It is in this context that Jesus shares his view of what it means to be 'blessed' or a 'saint' to his followers.

The Gospel reading draws our attention to something interesting. The Greek word *Makarios* that Jesus used means not just blessed, but a sense of deep-down happiness that stems from an intimacy with God, not the shallow happiness marketed by our society. Jesus did not tell them 'Look after yourselves, keep out of trouble and mind your own business … Stand up

122 William Stringfellow, *A Keeper of the Word: Selected Writings* (Grand Rapids, MI:Wm. B. Eerdmans,1996), p. 250.

only for your rights, and make trouble if you don't get them … don't worry about right and wrong … hope other people will be decent to you, regardless of how you treat them…compromise your principles to make life easy…' On the contrary, Jesus invites his followers to be content in heart, to be humble, to think of duty and service rather than self-interest, not intent on getting the better of other people, to hunger and thirst for righteousness. Jesus encourages them to be merciful, to be pure in heart, to be the peacemakers. In the light of the Beatitudes, saints are those who turn to Christ, look towards him and grow in his likeness, and in the process are drawn towards, and into, the lives and wellbeing of their fellow men and women.

Within the life of the Church, All Saints' Day celebrates those whose good examples remind us of what Jesus taught. The stories of the saints' ordinary lives remind us of who we are, what we believe, and what we can become. The saints inspire us not to lose sight of the ultimate goal: Jesus' imperative to love God with all our hearts and minds, and to love our neighbours as ourselves. Saints call us to an awareness of God's presence here and now. They help keep us from presuming too much about our own strength and enable us to think beyond our limitations. Saints lead us into the fullness of life that God intends for us all. Yes, saints are always different, in the sense of living a faith that results in actions that often fly in the face of a society that values individuality or self-interest. Saints become a divine corrective to loveless action and hatred.

As much as we long for a closer look at great souls from the past and the enduring example of their lives, we should not miss the saints of everyday. See them not just in the stained-glass windows but walking past us quietly. See them in retirement homes, speaking to the fragile ones in wheelchairs in the hallway. Hear them speaking peace and love amid the loud noises of hatred and fear. See them patiently helping vulnerable people in homeless shelters. See them serving food and giving a warm hug in food banks. See them in places ravaged by war and famine, providing food and medicine. See them in hospital emergency rooms, serving with skill and embracing with compassion, … you can also see them carefully cleaning the church, making coffee, arranging flowers, and washing the linens when nobody sees them. Saints were and are ordinary people like you and me, who show the love of God in their life and evoke a sense of God in us.

All Saints' Sunday is our day. This special day is for those who have been grasped by Christ, a day when we allow ourselves to be pierced by the gospel and be transformed. A day we share with the big-name saints and with those who have laboured in obscurity and silence, but who nevertheless within their own sphere of influence have repeatedly been witnesses to their living God by bringing hope. Today we are challenged by all the saints around us to match their obedience and dedication in our lives, here and now.

9

Attending to the Unspeakable: Last Words in Stone and Grief

FRANCES WARD

I postponed my dental appointment, told the playgroup leaders I'd drop in the following Friday instead, and washed the car that afternoon, scrubbing out the dog hairs and ingrained muck of years. That morning I'd taken the funeral of Emma. She'd died of leukaemia, very quickly, only just 17. The whole school was in shock. Her year at the local Church of England secondary school was large, and had crowded into church. The funeral service held us in a state of suspended animation with the comfort of hymns and prayers, poetry and music. We heard Christine Aguilera's 'Beautiful', and remembered Emma. The headteacher captured her life at school, bringing laughter to the tears.

I had preached. About how our lives are full of words, telling our stories. About our first words, when we are infants, and our last words. How some people always need to have the last word – but in fact there is never a last word, there's always more to be said. The conversations of our lives continue, even beyond death. I talked of her life as I'd heard it from family, the beauty of her personality, how dreadful was her loss. I talked of how she died; her courage and spirit. I said how gathering here today to remember Emma was to continue the conversation – that it might seem that her last word had been spoken, but that was not the case. I told the story of Mary Magdalene in the garden, and how she thought she had lost Jesus, the love of her life, on the cross, but through her tears she heard her name, and knew she was loved. How she experienced Jesus' love as he spoke her name; and how, since he died, and came back to life, he is the last word of love; a Word that never ends. Because Jesus is the Word of the God of love, our words of love continue through all time. Emma, now, is caught up into the conversation of eternal life and love, which is ours too, as we respond to the power of love.

Not in my own strength, I tried to speak the unspeakable, hold the unbearable. To shape this terrible experience within a reality that was abundantly more than we could think or imagine, and that framed our lives and deaths in the goodness and truth of a love that was eternal.

We walked, then – the whole school – down St Mary's Road to the cemetery. Alongside the undertaker in front of the hearse, this was the familiar road I walked every day, as I took my youngest children down the same road and through the same cemetery to their school. The road was strange this morning. My attention went to the usual places; but the usual things were out of place. Dogs that usually barked were silent. The faces that I would greet – Geoff and May – were not there, in their window, having their breakfast. Cars – which were few – drew to the curb and waited for us all to pass. We entered the cemetery. At some stage in the nineteenth century, local families had money to spend on large Victorian statues of angels cradling children, which captured well, despite the sentiment, an upward momentum in stone. One particular sculpture spoke, as not before, of the everlasting nature of grief yearning to hope.

When we reached the graveside, I called them all to gather around. We watched the coffin lowered in silence. I said the words, so familiar to me, so unfamiliar to all present, but comforting in the delivery as I carried my voice with confidence, willing each of those young people to know that death was not the final word.

The flowers, the letters, the teddy bears, the trinkets. All were left. No one was in any hurry to leave. Only gradually, gradually, did they head away in twos and threes, back to school, or to home, as this was a Friday afternoon.

I went home, and cleaned the car.

The following day, Saturday, I took the dog for a walk around the cemetery. The grave was a mountain of flowers. I paused to read the letters, poems, thoughts, reflections. So many of them – words continuing. And then, on Sunday, I visited Emma's mother. Her father was there too, even though they had separated; drawn together in their grief, for the sake of Emma's younger sister. 'We put her phone in with her,' said Mum. 'Just in case.' 'What, still switched on?' I exclaimed, despite myself. 'Yes. The battery will be dead by now.' I breathed fast and tried to calm myself as I imagined the phone ringing from the coffin, when we were gathered all around, and the impact that would have had on the assembly. I thanked God with all my heart that the phone hadn't had the last word.

No point in dwelling on that: I turned to Emma's sister, and asked how she was, and listened as she told me.

That was ten years ago. My oldest son was the same age as Emma was then, 17, so she would be 27 now. For some strange, unaccountable reason, she came back to mind as I prepared to preach for Remembrance Sunday 2018. Grief does that. It intensifies with the remembrance, or imagination, of other loss. Ten years ago, I was stirred not only by her death, but by my imagining if any of our children were to die. And at Remembrance, memory becomes viscous, compounded by the imagined memory of families, a century ago, who lost their 17-year-old sons on the Front. Grief solidifies, petrifies. Remembrance Sunday this year brought strong and poignant emotion, as I felt the unbearable loss of all mothers who have lost a child, particularly those near adulthood, and have had to live on. I recalled Emma's funeral as I stood there, and knew the sword that pierces the heart when your grown child dies, with a pain that is beyond words.

The sculpture of the angels with the child I grew to love, during the months after Emma's funeral. I understood the impulse to capture the grief in stone. I photographed it; tried to paint it, to capture the way the angels soared upwards, an unbearable lightness of the truth of love, from earthbound stone. Later on, I hated the *Doctor Who* episodes that featured stone angels as evil. I felt brutalized by the cynicism.

Now, Remembrance Sunday, we gathered around the town's memorial to the dead of 100 years ago. Brilliant, cold light, as the sun shone in the stillness of the air. The last post. Everyone held their breath, hoping that the young cornet player would keep her nerve and rise to the occasion, amid all the dignitaries and crowd. Two minutes expanded into an eternity.

Then the words of the Poet Laureate Carol Ann Duffy – a poem she'd written to mark the dying of Henry Allingham and Harry Patch, the two longest surviving soldiers from that war to end all wars. 'Last Post', with its image of the film spool running, telling the story towards the happy ending that never was. The last line of 'Last Post':

> If poetry could truly tell it backwards, then it would.[123]

From last word, to first, in honour of two soldiers remembered by name. I gazed at the sculpture of an unknown, unnamed man sitting, swinging to reach for his rifle, responding to a sense of duty and sacrifice that, we knew, was fraught with loss and waste. Wilfred Owen had captured the anonymity in his poem 'The Send Off'. How nameless soldiers went off, grimly gay, in trains to the Front:

> Shall they return to beatings of great bells
> In wild trainloads?

---

123 Carol Ann Duffy (ed.), *1914: Poetry Remembers* (London: Faber and Faber, 2013), pp. 112–3.

A few, a few, too few for drums and yells,
May creep back, silent, to still village wells
Up half-known roads.[124]

And in those years after 1918, by still village wells, went up statues that spoke of the heaviness of grief. No light, soaring angels here, but grief captured, the unspeakable loss of a generation immortalized in the middle of our communities. Living stones that marked a moment of national grief, and allowed life to go on because it must.

So why this tangle of grief, memory and reflection on words captured in poetry, sermon and stone? Perhaps because it is so hard to speak the unspeakable pain of human loss.

Rachel Mann's book *Fierce Imaginings* captures the complex legacies of World War One; how hard it is to remember, and yet how this war refuses to be forgotten. She writes of memorials and what they are designed to do. She speaks of how Christ is remembered in the Sacrament, but how Christ is never captured in stone or statue:

> The Christian re-membering of Christ is a constant practice of making 'present' and yet is a disappearing act. The embodiment of Christ in organic matter – in bread and wine – is a constant reinscription of fragility. Christ is not made to be cast in bronze or gold or stone like an idol. Christ is precisely not the Golden Calf.[125]

The lesson to be learned from this is just that: the statue of the unknown soldier invites contemplation of Jesus Christ, who will always be beyond our grasp, always pass our understanding. Our images of Christ-like figures, like those that hold the Great War

---

124 Wilfred Owen, 'The Send Off', in Carol Ann Duffy (ed.), *1914: Poetry Remembers* (London: Faber and Faber, 2013), pp. 4–5, first published in Wilfred Owen, *Poems*, ed. Siegfried Sassoon, (London: Chatto and Windus, 1921).

125 Rachel Mann, *Fierce Imaginings: The Great War, Ritual, Memory and God* (London: Darton, Longman and Todd, 2017),p. 25.

before our consciousness, will stir a sense of loss and sacrifice, with a judgement on the violence at the heart of the human condition. Mann describes how the Cenotaph fascinates her with the way 'it both mediates and points towards our civilisation's violence' (p. 27), obscuring and exposing the callousness that killed so many dead a century ago. Mann reminds us that we are brought face to face with our own humanity after a century in which we have been haunted, and continue to be haunted, by the image of young men who died, sacrificed to a sense of duty. Ours is a troubled consciousness shaped by modernity and postmodernity, empire and post-coloniality.

Gazing at the statue of the unknown soldier on that cold November morning, he was the young man who Carol Ann Duffy describes (not) coming home to warm beer and cricket, whose reality and innocence was shot through. He was the hero, the pal, the man who laid down his life for his friends, who went over the top through duty and fear. He was a reminder of useless, endless waste. He stirred in me desire. The desire of a mother, of a lover, of a sister, for what might have been. I became Mary Magdalene in that momentous two minutes.

Attending to unbearable loss takes me to Christ, who was and is the last Word of love that embraces all our transient, contingent words. Rowan Williams writes this: 'To speak of response is to gesture towards a prior reality of *address*, an address to which we are always "subsequent", even a gift which we are always seeking to receive appropriately.'[126] We are subsequent, and responding; we are also between the first and the last Word, caught in transience. Perhaps when we preach – whether in spoken word, action, stone angel, World War One memorial – we are trying to attend to the Word who is eternally present, who holds us in goodness and truth through all loss and grief.

As I prepare to preach, and deliver the sermon, I prayerfully

126 Rowan Williams, *The Edge of Words: God and the Habits of Language* (London: Bloomsbury, 2014), p. 33.

attend to Christ, the living Christ, crucified and risen. I repeat the words *Ecce Homo* quietly, meditatively, as I prepare, as I stand in the pulpit, ready to begin. I attend to the man who is the Word of God, the last word of love who lives for ever, who holds all our words of grief, expressions of loss, art and performance and makes them bear God's grace.

This encounter has real power to transform. When Saul travelled the road to Damascus, was blinded by light, fell to the ground and heard a voice, he asked 'Who are you, Lord?' The reply came, 'I am Jesus'. Saul, at that point, was called into being and began to give himself to the Lord (Acts 22.6–9). His subjectivity, and name, changed for ever. He encountered the living Christ, and was transformed. At the heart of every sermon is this encounter; a movement between Christ and the human subject, a movement of grace given and received, a Word spoken that stirs response and change. A rapport of love that makes a sermon sacramental; that equips the Christian disciple to go into the world in peace to love and serve the Lord.

To say *Ecce Homo* is to speak the unspeakable. Christ the Word of God is not contained by our words. There is always more; and into that 'more' our words are endless as we try to capture the glory of God, the divine, and the profundity of human loss and grief that can only find itself on the cross. Our endless words include those sculpted in stone as figures such as the unknown soldier who prompts an *Ecce Homo* moment, pointing to Christ and to the crucifixion. Things – life – continues because Christ took the finality of death with him to the cross, enabling us to say 'O Death, where is your sting? O Grave, where is your victory?'

It's an affirmation of faith that is true as we affirm it, though it doesn't depend on our affirmation. We affirm it by attention to the *Ecce Homo* who is there in the World War One memorial on Remembrance Sunday, in stone angels, in all the sermons that offer an encounter with the living Christ, who is life and love at the depth of suffering and loss, in the waste of young life gone.

We were there on Remembrance Sunday, gathered in our humility, attending to a story that holds each of us in a drama that is greater than any the human being can conceive, brought face to face with the story of Christianity, the unspeakable loss of the cross. The statue of the unknown soldier was an offer to look at the sacrifice of Christ on the cross and to struggle with the need to forgive, to refuse the impulse for revenge.

Some 30 short years before the end of World War One, between 15 October and 4 November 1888, two years before he died, and a year before he was confirmed insane, Friedrich Nietzsche wrote a short summation of his philosophy, *Ecce Homo: How One Becomes What One Is*. In it he presents the figure of Zarathustra.

> Ah, you men, I see an image sleeping in the stone, the image of my visions! Ah, that it must sleep in the hardest, ugliest stone!
> *Now my hammer rages fiercely against its prison*. Fragments fly from the stone: what is that to me?
> I will complete it: for a shadow came to me – the most silent, the lightest of all things came to me!
> The beauty of the superman came to me as a shadow: what are the gods to me now![127]

Nietzsche was determined to turn over what he saw as the malign sickness of Christianity. It's almost as if he foresaw the sacrifice of World War One as he argued that Christ's self-sacrifice was servile and despicable, fostering a mean-minded herd mentality in Christians. Weak and pathetic, Christians used manipulative means to exert themselves, exhibiting their own all-too-human selfish needs as they seek to meet the needs of others. He had no time for Christ and Christianity; he wrote, instead, of the anti-Christ. He uses the title *Ecce Homo* deliberately and ironically: 'Behold the man!' Zarathustra is the man now – humanity come

127 Friedrich Nietzsche, *Ecce Homo: How One Becomes What One Is*, trans. with introduction by R. J. Hollingdale (Harmondsworth and New York: Penguin [1888] 1979), p. 110.

into its own, leaving behind this snivelling morality of Christianity, and looking down from the heights of self-assertion and the mastery of the will to power.

He turns to the Greek god Dionysos – the god of self-determination and joyful chaos (whom he contrasts with Apollo – the God of order and rule). His understanding of Dionysos informs his prophetic character Zarathustra – who is his archetype for the superman. Zarathustra overturns the old morality of Christianity, based on selflessness, and asserts the self as the glorious being who has the will to power to conquer the earth. Zarathustra is beyond good and evil; he has affected the transvaluation of value and inaugurated a new realm where the human rules supreme. This is the Man (Nietzsche had no time for women, who, he believed, were weak and manipulative), who stands against the world, against the elements, who has left behind the need to serve others. This superman follows his own fate – *amor fati* – loving his fate, his destiny, following it into lonely but glorious self-assertion. *Ecce Homo!* Nietzsche's *Ecce Homo* challenges the impulse that carried away so many young men across Europe to die for love of their country. He would have hated the statues to the unknown soldier. Nietzsche's *Ecce Homo* ends with the words ('Have I been understood? – *Dionysos against the Crucified …*').

His achievement was breathtaking, and his re-valuation of values is known in all aspects of culture, thought, history – all that influences Western society today. When Pilate remonstrated with the Jews in the Gospel of John (19.5), '*Ecce Homo!*' he said. The Christ who stood before him was the very antipathy of Nietzsche's man. He was weak, beaten, condemned to die, and accepting his fate without resentment or resistance. Such, thought Nietzsche, deserved only contempt. He hated the way Christians manipulated others by weakness and controlling need. Instead, Dionysos offered the strength of a life lived to the lees, with glorious embrace of all darkness and light.

As today's preacher seeks the words to convey the word of

God, she needs to commend Christ into a culture and society that has, 120 years after Nietzsche published *Ecce Homo*, absorbed the re-valuation of values and the contempt for Christ that Nietzsche taught. Nietzsche refuses to be taken literally. He uses words by turns provocative, aphoristic, hyperbolic. He is deadly serious, though, in his war on Christianity. The sort of 'man' that results from Christianity earns only Nietzsche's contempt: '… they are the refuse of mankind, abortive offspring of sickness and revengeful instincts: they are nothing but pernicious, fundamentally incurable monsters who take revenge on life'.[128] He styles himself as the *Anti-Christ*.[129] With the Anti-Christ, Nietzsche offers a wild affirmation of life, a profound contrast to Christian morality, with its emphasis on self-denial, sacrifice and duty, a Christianity that had killed the best in humanity. Nietzsche presents a 'life' that has such potency it can be thought to recur eternally.

Nietzsche's words have had tremendous appeal. His repudiation of Christ and contempt for the morality that commends self-sacrifice, duty and the acceptance of suffering caught fire after World War One, and continues to capture the imagination of many today.

To attend to '*Ecce Homo!*' – Behold, the Man! – is to ask ourselves what humanity is. Here preaching becomes deeply countercultural as it seeks an encounter with the Christ who holds all that is unspeakable, the depths of loss and grief. It is to witness to the absence, the death of death.

We must be careful with our words, for they might preach the presence of a different human, the Nietzschean anti-Christ, a new humanity that finds itself in the affirmation of itself, powerful with a strong life that denied the self-sacrificial way of Christ. Nietzsche's prophetic words affirmed a humanity without limit. Our words can do this, and often do. Or the preacher can find words to attend to the Christ who invites us

128 Nietzsche, *Ecce Homo*, p. 67.
129 Nietzsche, *Ecce Homo*, p. 72.

towards life lived not alone but with others, deeply engaged in the community, not contemptuous of 'the herd' of the ordinary people around, who face into the depths of grief and loss seeking God's grace and life. To respond to this invitation is to recognize that our words will never capture Christ, but will stretch themselves to speak the unspeakable in the trust and knowledge that love is the final word that Jesus revealed.

What is the *Ecce Homo* that I preach? A question for all preachers. As I've attempted to answer, I've considered angels in stone, the statues of unknown soldiers, the stone sculpture of Zarathustra that Nietzsche imagined himself carving – all sermons of one sort or another. I've been taken back to the funeral of a 17-year-old young woman who died before her time. I've spoken of the experience of grief and loss that folds over, in time and through history, with all the horror and depth of a mud-filled trench, a grave in a cemetery in a town in Lancashire, and how our words cannot express the dense and intractable extremes of human life and death; our words are always inadequate, never enough, without attention to the *Ecce Homo* who is present in every sermon.

I might have preached any number of sermons at Emma's funeral. The one most tempting would have summoned the young people to become what they are. To affirm their lives in the face of Emma's death; to live life fully by seeking to realize their potential; to aspire to self-fulfilment in her name and memory. Such a sermon would have validated and celebrated, in Nietzschean spirit, the unique person Emma was. With a focus on her and each young person present in their specialness, it would have amounted to a refusal to let her go. Paradoxically, she would have become the final word; the words would have exhausted themselves, and dried up, much as the battery of the mobile phone eventually went dead.

Instead, I attended to a reality in which we participate, and in which we never come to an end. Within that reality, we reach the edge of words, caught up in the ineffable nature of God.

Our words in sermon and poetry – and stone statue – are never enough to comprehend that reality. Only as we attend to the incarnate Word that is Jesus Christ do our words find their place. The Word that is Christ gives continuity to experience so we can carry on, responding and attending as we encounter the living Lord, who is as faithful as the love of God, and in whom we are held, enabled to grow and flourish eternally.

> So Jesus came out, wearing the crown of thorns and the purple robe.
> Pilate said to them, 'Here is the man!' (John 19.5)

A Sermon for the Feast of Christ the King: The Alpha and the Omega

Victoria Johnson, accompanied by Edmund Aldhouse (Assistant Organist, Ely Cathedral)

There was once a sound of the most unimaginable purity, a sound of the most staggering clarity and beauty – a sound of the most perfect truth.

(A single note sounds from the organ)

The sound was there before anything else, the first of all things, a perfect singularity.

From the resonance of the sound all manner of things came into being – dust and matter emanated from its core, stars were flung into space, galaxies spun into position, supernova were thrown into existence and the embryos of billions of planets were set on their course.

(There are sparkles of notes glimmering from the organ)

The sound expanded. The sound was persistent, it did not flicker, or waver, it never stopped even for a nano-second, whatever that might mean in a universe without measure. As time came into existence the sound evolved, it wasn't just a sound any more, it was a note – as clear as the day.

(The sound gets louder, other notes join in)

Cosmologists, and those who study these things, say the note is in fact a B flat – 57 octaves below middle C.

(The lowest note on the organ is played, it rumbles around the cathedral)

The universe was humming from the very beginning and began to gather other notes until the notes became music.

(The organist improvises, but beneath everything is the one note)

In a corner of this universe, a rocky globe was growing into its vocation. It was gathering speed and spinning through space – it was battered and bruised by colliding comets and asteroids. It was stretched and shaped, and cracked, and moulded. It was waking from its slumber as it circled the brightest of lights, its cold and icy centre was melting.

On its surface there was a stream of fire, molten lava and explosions, vast plates were being formed and from these growing pains there came something of the likeness of land and sea, a crystal river, the water of life from which life emerged. With all the noise it was difficult to hear anything, but if you listened carefully there was that note, clear and bright and true at the foundation of all things.

The symphony of creation itself was taking shape and everything that was created had the capacity to echo the sound of the most perfect truth, the song of the universe, which was from the beginning.

But the sound needed a voice – the music was yearning to be embodied in flesh and blood and at last – into this bundle of life – came song, in something like the sound of a crying baby. It was a song of the most imaginable purity, the most staggering clarity – the sound of the most perfect truth.

(The music stops)

Over 2,000 years ago there was a conversation – a conversation after a betrayal, which would turn the world on its axis. A conversation to reveal the truth that had been humming in the universe from its inception.

The proud and powerful of this earth had come to think that they had the first and the last word in everything; they lauded themselves and sat on their thrones; they pronounced judgement without wisdom and without mercy and they thought they were gods. They couldn't hear the sound of the universe; they couldn't hear its truth – because their ears were full of their own importance. But remember, the sound had become a voice and the voice now spoke from human lips.

The voice said, 'My Kingdom is not from this world.'

'So you are a king?' Pilate asked him.

Jesus answered: 'You say that I am a king. For this I was born, and for this I came into the world, to testify to the truth. Everyone who belongs to the truth, listens to my voice.'

What kind of king was this?

Rulers, principalities and powers would be floored by him. He would burst the bubble of all small-minded pomp. With clarity he would interrogate those who put their faith in riches and those who trampled on the innocent.

But those with ears to hear would be exalted; the humble, the weak, the poor, the downcast, the small, they could hear his voice and they began to sing. Even those who were thought to be dead would hear him calling and walk out of their tombs. His Kingdom, was not of this world; his Kingdom was changing the world and its assumptions for ever. The pure sound of his voice was able to crack the glass hearts of those whose universe had shrunk to the size of their own self.

But the conversation had consequences, and this strange king was nailed to a cross and wore a crown of thorns.

What kind of king was this?

He was more like a lamb led to the slaughter. With the sound of each nail being hammered through his flesh into wood, the universe trembled, the earth began to shake, and the sky turned black.

(A single note sounds from the organ)

Early in the morning, just before dawn as the birds sang innocently in the garden, a sound could be heard.

A sound so pure, and clear and true it was unmistakable. The sound had never stopped. It wasn't just a sound, it was a note as clear as the day, something of the likeness of a B flat but we can't be sure, and then it was a voice, and then it was a song and then the whole universe joined in this hymn of praise.

The song continued. It continues still. Can you hear it?

(The organist improvises)

One day, the day we are all waiting for, this King, not of this world, will come again with the clouds of heaven and all peoples and languages and nations will behold, every eye shall see him and they will hear his voice, they will join in with his song, they will be swept up by his music. With majesty like no other he is the one who was, and who is, and who is to come.

The ancient one, forever made new, will take to his throne and a stream of fire will flow from his presence, burning up injustice, hatred and sin and his kingship shall never be destroyed. 'So it is to be', creation sings. Amen and Amen.

Christ is King, not only of our hearts, not only in our worship, not only in the Church, not only of this world. Christ is King of the universe, over all things, in all things, above all things. The ground of our being. The song that never stops. The truth above all truths who comes to dwell with us, so in this feast we can hold the universe in our hands, and taste and see.

Suffer us not to make our vision of his power and glory too small. Christ is the power beyond all power, the glory of all glories, the love of all loves, the Alpha and the Omega, the beginning and the end – and we and the whole created order are called to worship at his feet.

So it is to be. Amen and Amen.

(The improvisation draws to a close into a single note – a sound that was from the beginning.)

Afterword: Preachers as Artisans

PAULA GOODER

The authors in this book have explored and celebrated the art of preaching. In fact, at various points throughout the volume the word 'craft' has been used to describe the process both of writing and of delivering sermons. This image of preaching as 'craft' is important. No craftsperson learns their craft overnight. It is true that some people are more naturally gifted in some areas than others are, but the best craftspeople are those who have practised, experimented, made mistakes, tried again and, after hours and hours of honing their skill, become expert. The very best craftspeople never stop learning. They continue to tinker and discover new ways of doing what they already do well.

Preaching, similarly, is a skill that can be learnt. As with all crafts, some people are naturally gifted preachers but, whether they come naturally or not, the skills of preaching, from writing to delivering sermons, can be learnt, reflected on and improved. It is worth noting that the skills of preaching fall into three main areas: the reflection stage (engaging with Scripture and drawing ideas together); the composition stage (the actual writing of the sermon); and the proclamation stage (delivering the sermon). All three stages have their own skill sets that need developing and honing, though, inevitably, the wisdom contained in a book such as this contributes more to the first two stages than the final one.

My grandad was a cabinet maker and I remember, as a child,

watching him as he turned an old, dusty – usually reclaimed and unwanted – piece of wood into a beautiful French-polished piece of furniture. My grandad was a craftsperson, but he was a frustrated craftsperson: he was born at the wrong time. Although he produced the most beautiful pieces of furniture, he had the misfortune of having been born early in the twentieth century when mass-produced, machine-crafted furniture was coming into fashion. Throughout his life he apologized for the beautiful woodwork he produced, assuming that we would have preferred something more off-the-shelf and fashionable.

Fortunately, craft is, slowly, making a resurgence. The early twenty-first century has seen the recovery of a love of well-made, slowly–produced, locally–crafted items, whether they be furniture, beer or bread; cakes, cheese or other handicrafts. The pre-fix 'artisan' or 'artisanal' capitalizes on this renewed interest and aims to make such items sound more attractive than would the simple description 'homemade'. The word 'artisan' may be over-used but it indicates the presence of finely honed ability. An artisan is highly skilled and makes things by hand using traditional methods. An artisan is also, often, locally based, using locally sourced ingredients in the finished product.

'Artisanal' is a word that fits particularly well with preaching. Sermons are, by their nature, artisanal. They require skill. They call us back to traditional methods of exegesis, reflection and application. Composing them takes time, often a lot of time, and crucially they are profoundly local: comprising what God has to say in this place, at this time.

For many years the craft of preaching appeared to be dying out in parts of Great Britain. It wasn't that it wasn't done or done very well. There were, and are still, many highly skilled preachers throughout the country, but preaching as a craft was not often celebrated, or indeed widely discussed and explored. Theological colleges and courses fell back on teaching the practicalities of preaching and often made the evaluation of sermons the main focus of their teaching. Few courses, colleges or courses laid on lengthy modules on homiletics, such as can be found in seminaries in the USA. Having said this, there has been in recent years a resurgence of interest in preaching. Indeed, the popularity of the Festival of Preaching in Oxford, held first in 2017 and again in 2019, gives testimony to the rekindling of interest in the craft itself. This recovery of interest in preaching is welcome. For a while now, a number of people have relished the potential demise of the sermon, declaring it to be defunct: an outmoded form of communication best replaced by other more up-to-date techniques. While they may not be completely wrong – it is always good to explore the most effective modes of communication for contemporary audiences – it is high time that we revisit the task of preaching itself and ask what skills make a sermon most effective.

Of course, the problem with discussing the craft of preaching is that it can induce guilt in already busy preachers. Many preachers are so busy in other areas of life that it can be hard to give the time that we might want to the writing of a sermon. Discussing preaching skills can be felt to imply that what you are doing is just not good enough. This is not what reflecting on the craft of preaching is about. There is no 'perfect sermon'; improvements can always be made, no matter how early you start, and the temptation to tweak your script even as you ascend the pulpit steps can sometimes be overwhelming. Reflections on the craft of preaching are not – and should not be – focused on critiquing a particular sermon and declaring it 'good' or 'bad', 'effective' or 'ineffective', 'adequate' or 'inadequate' – as any preacher will tell you God can speak through even the worst and least eloquent of our efforts. Exploring the craft of preaching, instead, requires us to think about preaching as a set of skills and about building up a range of abilities that will shape and inspire preaching in the future.

Something that sticks vividly in my mind about my grandad is that whenever he saw a piece of furniture, which to his eye looked to be well-made, he would examine it minutely, pulling out his notebook to jot down what he learnt. He would, to my granny's great shame, even pull it away from the wall to look at the joints on the back, so he could see how it had been put together. His delight in dovetail joints or well-executed veneers was a joy to behold.

It is sometimes said that collections of sermons are pointless. Sermons are preached in a particular place, at a particular time, to a particular group of people. It is argued that as soon as you remove their particularity, then their power is also removed. This may be true, at least in part, but there is another point to collections of sermons that remains significant. Sermons – such as the ones in this collection – allow us to do the equivalent of my grandad's pulling out the furniture and looking at the back. Most people who preach hear largely their own sermons, and sometimes those of a handful of others. This does not allow for good reflection on the craft of preaching. We need the chance to savour other people's sermons, to look at how they were put together, and to reflect on what can be learnt for our own preaching. This book, unusually, intersperses chapters on preaching with actual sermons and, in doing so, encourages us even more to reflect on the skills involved in the preparation of sermons.

One of the other memories I have of my grandad was his absorption in what he was creating. There was a quality to his attention, a focused immersion in the task at hand that drew you in. I used to be sent to summon him to dinner, though this was never an easy task. His attention to his craft was so all-consuming that it took time to redirect his interest to mundane necessities like eating.

Another of the important strands in this book is the strand of attentiveness. Attentiveness – to Scripture, to God's people, to time and place and, most importantly, to God – lies at the heart of the craft of preaching. This attentiveness, which begins during the time of preparation and finds its culmination in proclamation, is what makes preaching such a profound experience.

One of the challenges for preachers is to show their attentiveness both in what they say and in how they say it. Absorption is catching. I remember being drawn into my grandad's own absorption as I watched him. Telling people to 'pay attention' or 'be attentive' is far less effective than showing them what attentiveness looks like in practice. This is something that cannot be captured in one sermon, or seen in one act of preaching. There is a longevity to the attentiveness of preaching that needs to be laid out week after week, month after month, year after year, until its character can be caught. We live in a quick-fix, consumerist world. Preaching is the ultimate in 'slow-food' – in this case slow-spiritual-food – a nourishment to the soul, a way of being, that shapes us deep within.

I remember an exchange in the *Church Times* letters page a few years ago in which someone was espousing the familiar case of the futility of preaching on the grounds that the correspondent could not remember any of the sermons that he had heard over a number of years of being in church. His respondent said simply that over his lifetime he had eaten many dinners. He could not, now, remember what they were, he said, but he was alive. The dinners had nourished him and given him life. His point was powerful. Some sermons are noteworthy and memorable but many are simply nourishing. They form not only the preacher but the hearers too into a new way of being that finds its roots in attentiveness and its branches in action.

This reminds us of a fourth, and crucial, stage of the craft of preaching: the living it out. We should never forget that preaching lives on in the lives of those who hear it. Really good preaching shapes not just what we think for the duration of the sermon or the service but how we live our lives in the weeks and months that follow. In other words, the afterlife of a sermon is as important as its time in preparation and composition. This has not been the focus of this book, whose focus rightly has been on earlier stages of the preaching process. Perhaps one day, however, a similar volume on the latter stages of the process (including how congregations best engage with, receive and live out the preaching they hear) might be welcomed.

This collection of essays on preaching and sermons is important, not just for the wisdom it contains, but because it reminds us of the importance of preaching as a craft: a craft that can be learnt and that requires practice and skill. Holy attention lies at the heart of this craft, both for those who preach and for those who hear the preaching and live it out. The craft of preaching summons preachers to the life of an artisan: to a life of learning, of reflection, and of experimentation – but most of all to a life of attentiveness. In other words, preaching is a whole-life activity and takes a lifetime to learn.

Index of Names and Subjects

and the significance of the building, my experience of preaching that day was as if all [illegible] plus of us were in an intimate space. Yes, I projected, I performed, I deployed all sorts of rhetorical tricks and tropes, but in the midst of [illegible] it was as if we stepped outside of the ordered space (and time) into one that was more startling. It was as if we were eyeball-to-eyeball and we were not afraid. Generally, one has no desire to be so intimate with anyone unless it is with one's lover. Yet I sensed it was where I was called to be; I sensed others were there with me. There was, in the intense dynamic of preaching, strangeness and intimacy. There was embodied grace. It is to what I mean by this that I want to now turn.

What else happened?

A sermon might appear to be many things. If one were to pick up a collection of sermons – perhaps the sort of erudite collections considered suitable for the instruction of well-heeled, white ladies in a Jane Austen novel – one might suggest that a sermon comprises a set of words on a page sealed safely inside calf's skin. It is, on this kind of picture, an anachronistic object of power and cultural formation. A collection of sermons might be read as a gathering-up of ancient power and authority, perhaps rendered safe and saleable for the genteel to consume privately. Indeed, one might claim that those 'classic' leather-bound, eighteenth- and nineteenth-century collections of sermons are metonymic for authorized, white, middle-class, clerical power.

Equally, one might read the notion of sermon and preaching through the language of art. When we, at Manchester Cathedral, established the Manchester Sermon as a secular literary series in [illegible], the invitation letter I composed contained this: 'Many of the nation's greatest poets and thinkers, from Donne through to Newman, have used the sermon as a place for pushing the boundaries of English and reflecting upon what it means to be human. Dr Johnson famously noted, "that sermons